UNESCO on the Ground

ENCOUNTERS: Explorations in Folklore and Ethnomusicology
A *Journal of Folklore Research* Book

UNESCO on the Ground

Local Perspectives on Intangible Cultural Heritage

Edited by Michael Dylan Foster and Lisa Gilman

INDIANA UNIVERSITY PRESS

Bloomington and Indianapolis

This book is a publication of

Indiana University Press
Office of Scholarly Publishing
Herman B Wells Library 350
1320 East 10th Street
Bloomington, Indiana 47405 USA

iupress.indiana.edu

The paper used in this publication meets the minimum requirements of
the American National Standard for Information Sciences—Permanence
of Paper for Printed Library Materials, ANSI Z39.48-1992.

Manufactured in the United States of America

Library of Congress Control Number: 2015948433

1 2 3 4 5   21 20 19 18 17 16

On the cover: Inventory of Intangible Cultural Heritage of Northern Malawi by Malawi
National Commission of UNESCO and Malawi Department of Culture (Museums
of Malawi). Iponga, Karonga District. February 9, 2014. Courtesy of Lisa Gilman.

Contents

UNESCO on the Ground

UNESCO on the Ground

The practices, representations, expressions, knowledge, skills—as well as the instruments, objects, artefacts and cultural spaces associated therewith—that communities, groups and, in some cases, individuals recognize as part of their cultural heritage.

—UNESCO, 2003 *Convention for the Safeguarding of the Intangible Cultural Heritage*

THESE WORDS ARE invoked by the United Nations Educational, Scientific, and Cultural Organization, commonly known as UNESCO, to define the term *intangible cultural heritage* or, in the current academic-bureaucratic vernacular, *ICH*.[1] UNESCO's language here is open-ended, if not vague, but clearly includes the sort of expressive culture long studied by folklorists. Significantly, the definition emphasizes recognition of ICH on the *local* level, by the "communities," "groups," and "individuals" involved with the practices, representations, expressions, knowledge, and skills under consideration. I note here the importance of the local in this definition, and indeed in much of UNESCO's ICH discourse, because of the potential disconnect between this massive international organization headquartered in Paris and the disparate small communities scattered throughout the globe targeted by its efforts and affected by its decisions. It is perhaps inevitable that UNESCO's metacultural policies often become a testing ground for negotiations between the global and the local (however defined) and all points in between, where responses can be highly nuanced and often contentious.

Decisions made in distant cities influence national, regional, and local discourses on everything from economic development and tourism to racial conflict and depopulation. They illuminate, and also

1

potentially exacerbate, all sorts of political, ethnic, and ideological divisions in places where ICH is not just a matter of theory but part of everyday life. The essays in this volume examine several such places through case studies in India, South Korea, Malawi, Japan, Macedonia, and China. Each explores how people involved with and affected on the ground by ICH initiatives experience, perceive, and respond to UNESCO and related entities.

In recent years, UNESCO and ICH have become key terms for the analysis of expressive culture, with folklorists involved in the theorization, creation, and implementation of global cultural policy and also offering critical analyses of such policies and of the role of UNESCO as an arbiter of culture.[2] In 2012, a collection of essays entitled *Heritage Regimes and the State* (Bendix, Eggert, and Peselmann 2012a) provided an invaluable extended comparative examination of the ways in which UNESCO's current heritage policy has been implemented within individual nations. The chapters in that study bring to the fore the diversity of traditions that come under the purview of UNESCO's ICH umbrella and also illustrate the diversity of bureaucratic structures through which elements are nominated for recognition, policies are implemented, and "heritage" is maintained and (re)created.

We hope the case studies presented here will add to this groundbreaking work through their focus on the particularly intimate perspectives of people living in communities touched by ICH policies. Without overlooking the interests of national and regional stakeholders, our essays are informed primarily by individuals grappling on a grassroots level with the practical ramifications of UNESCO decisions in places where heritage is not an abstract concept but a mode of quotidian practice. In the words of Kristin Kuutma (2012, 33), "Research on communities will penetrate deeper if investigated as particularities." And indeed, it is exactly these particularities that the essays here investigate, especially the manifold ways in which local residents participate in, respond to, and shape UNESCO (and other) cultural policies within their own communities. Our case studies explore how international designations and decisions affect (or do not affect) residents' everyday lives and relationships, economic structures, senses of identity, and engagement with their own cultural practices.

In short, the objective of this collection is first and foremost to tap into local discourses and to present the voices, experiences, and ideas of people living in places where ICH is a topic of concern. It is in this sense that we invoke the term *local*: in part because it suggests an opposite or complementary perspective to the *global*, but more importantly because of its emphasis on specific *places*. That is, the local does not necessarily indicate the size or population or type of community (another vexed word in the current discourse), but it does invoke a sense of place, of locale or location.[3] We are interested in the situation and opinions and agency of the people residing on site, "in place" as it were, in distinction to people in regional or national capitals, for example, or more distant locales in other countries. We recognize that such distinctions are always blurry—that people and ideas travel. A power broker in a small village, for instance, may also play a role within regional or national contexts, and, inversely, an individual working on a regional or national level may maintain direct connections with much smaller communities.[4] But accepting this fuzziness, our focus is on the site and the people who reside there.

I should add also that when we say *local*, of course, we really mean *locals*, and that within each one of these locals there exist different social divisions, power differentials, and other dimensions of diversity, further complicating the constitution of what is "local." Through case studies in different parts of the world, we highlight such critical differences and similarities between distinct places and communities and provide material for comparative analysis. By exploring each of these sites at a micro level, looking outward from the inside, we show how a "normative instrument" (Aikawa 2004) such as UNESCO's ICH policy takes on specific associations and inflections. By providing individual examples—and the particular issues that inform different local discourses—for comparison and contrast, we can explore the practical implications of UNESCO's work. We see our own comparative project here as part of a long tradition of folklorists paying careful attention to the complexities of local situations.[5]

Metacultural and Esocultural

Barbara Kirshenblatt-Gimblett (2004, 56) has insightfully described heritage as "metacultural" and lists of the type created by UNESCO as "metacultural artefects." Kuutma (2012, 24) notes that "the metacultural is inevitably turned into or embraced by the cultural." With this in mind, the essays here explore the ways metaculture intervenes in culture. Or taking this one step further, perhaps what we are really trying to unpack is something even tighter, more localized, and more limited—the microcultural or, to coin a term, the *esocultural*, with the prefix *eso-* suggesting "within" in contrast to the "above" and "beyond" of *meta-*.

If metacultural operations can sometimes run the risk of missing the trees for the forest, then our own project represents a conscious effort to burrow into the foliage of particular cultures, communities, and places to discover the trees themselves. And what we learn through this effort is that different forests are constituted in different ways, that not all trees are equal, and that not all trees have the same relationship to the forest in which they are located. To extend the metaphor even further, what is driven home to us along with the diversity of individual trees is the range of soils and climates and the many other elements that create the environment in which they grow. Ultimately, it is this tree-level perspective, replete with its own biases and diversity and limits, that we want to capture—the ways UNESCO and similar global actors may be interpreted, understood, ignored, or even completely unknown by actors on the esocultural level. Such on-the-ground perceptions are colored with details of place and personal relationships that are often invisible from the bird's-eye view of UNESCO or the academic-bureaucratic heritage industrial complex (of which we too are inevitably a part). These are the rough edges and loose ends, the personalities and peculiarities of place, that often go unobserved when looking from a distance at national or global "heritage-scapes" (Di Giovine 2009). But it is exactly this closeness and these details, the agency of people in place, that we want to learn from here. The essays assembled in the pages that follow demonstrate that each unique esocultural perspective, with its inherent limitations, not only sheds light on metacultural perspectives but also ultimately highlights the mutually constitutive nature of the metacultural and esocultural as optics for viewing that notoriously elusive concept called "culture."

The Convention and the Representative List

The policy instrument that inspired this collection of essays was adopted by the General Conference of UNESCO in October 2003. The Convention for the Safeguarding of the Intangible Cultural Heritage was actually only the most recent in a long series of UNESCO policies concerning heritage, of both the "tangible" and "intangible" varieties.

The most influential earlier policy was the Convention Concerning the Protection of the World Cultural and Natural Heritage (1972), which introduced the World Heritage List, "a great public relations coup for UNESCO and . . . no doubt what the organisation is best known for in many parts of the world" (Hafstein 2009, 95).

While this 1972 Convention concerns *tangible* heritage—architectural structures, monuments, natural and cultural landscapes, etc.—UNESCO also began developing instruments for treating more amorphous, nonmaterial products and processes of culture. The Recommendation on the Safeguarding of Traditional Culture and Folklore was promulgated in 1989, followed by the Proclamation of Masterpieces of the Oral and Intangible Heritage of Humanity approved in 1998 (with the first proclamation in 2001). The ICH Convention of 2003 builds on these earlier instruments, but as a "Convention" (in distinction to a "Recommendation" or "Proclamation") it represents a stronger, legally binding, standard-setting instrument.[6] In theory, this means that a national signatory to the Convention is technically in violation of international law if it fails to "take the necessary measures to ensure the safeguarding of the intangible cultural heritage present in its territory" (Article 11[a]); in practice, however, no sanctions for such a violation have been stipulated (Sano 2005, 371).[7]

The negotiations leading to the inception of the 2003 Convention were complex and contentious on both practical and theoretical levels (Aikawa 2004; Kurin 2004; Miyata 2007; Aikawa-Faure 2009; Hafstein 2009). One end product of these discussions was a system whereby individual "states parties" (nations) could submit an "element" (ICH) for "inscription" (inclusion) on a newly established Representative List of the Intangible Cultural Heritage of Humanity. Determining the criteria and parameters for this Representative List proved among "the most controversial issues" of the 2003 ICH Convention negotiations (Hafstein 2009, 93).[8] It goes without saying that any kind of list is potentially problematic (Kirshenblatt-Gimblett 2004; Hafstein 2009); with so many different stakeholders involved and so much potentially eligible ICH, a global inventory of this nature certainly risks interpretation (or manipulation) as a political tool of exclusion, privilege, or control. Moreover, selection for a list inevitably recontextualizes a tradition and can alter the way a given practice is understood by its practitioners.

The term *representative* itself is problematic, or at least paradoxical: in theory a representative may be chosen for its quality of being "average" or "typical." But as the most clearly defined example within a particular category of things, a "representative" is inevitably anything but average or typical, and its very selection *as* representative removes it from the fold, elevating it above or at least distinguishing it from others. From UNESCO's metacultural global vantage point, a selected element may be just one of many on a list, but from the perspective of the culture, state, or community it represents, the element occupies a singularly vaunted position in contrast to all the other elements that were not selected. A representative is *primus inter pares*.

Even within UNESCO institutional discourse, *representative* is open to interpretation. Early on, the understanding was that UNESCO would simply accept submissions from States Parties so "the list would be comprised of traditional cultures that each state considers 'representative' of itself" (Sano 2005, 377). Gradually, however, this interpretation morphed into one in which UNESCO itself became more active in the selection process in order to create a list that would represent "cultural diversity" in terms of geography as well as genre (378). Given this (re)interpretation, the selection of representatives becomes a tool through which UNESCO shapes a heritage landscape to conform to its own metacultural visions.

Having said this, however, it is also important to recognize that the Representative List is "an outcome of a cultural relativist perspective influenced by postmodernist trends" (Kuutma 2012, 29) and reflects a conscious attempt by the formulators of the Convention to create a more egalitarian and inclusive inscription process. The List developed from earlier policy instruments, such as the Proclamation of the Masterpieces of the Oral and Intangible Heritage of Humanity, for which individual states would submit a single nomination every two years to be carefully reviewed for proclamation as a "Masterpiece" (see Seeger 2009): "a space or form of cultural expression . . . of outstanding value" (UNESCO 2000).[9] By 2005, a total of ninety Masterpieces had been proclaimed. When the Convention took effect in 2008, these ninety elements became the foundation of the newly established Representative List.

While the Masterpieces proclamation required a "cultural expression or cultural space" to demonstrate "outstanding value as a masterpiece of the human creative genius" (UNESCO 2001, 12), the 2003 Convention was carefully crafted to avoid the rhetoric of elite judgment. In particular the adjective "representative" was invoked in part to "add the nuance that elements on the list would be examples of intangible cultural heritage of the whole world" (Sano 2005, 377), and the Director-General of UNESCO at the time explained that "the notion of 'outstanding universal significance' was deliberately excluded from the Convention" (Matsuura 2007, 179). In contrast, ICH was defined as

> the practices, representations, expressions, knowledge, skills—as well as the instruments, objects, artefacts and cultural spaces associated therewith—that communities, groups and, in some cases, individuals recognize as part of their cultural heritage. This intangible cultural heritage, transmitted from generation to generation, is constantly recreated by communities and groups in response to their environment, their interaction with nature and their history, and provides them with a sense of identity and continuity, thus promoting respect for cultural diversity and human creativity. (UNESCO 2003, 2)

In 2008, the ninety "Masterpieces" were transferred to the Representative List, and then in 2009, UNESCO's ICH Committee convened in Abu Dhabi to inscribe the "first elements" (UNESCO 2009). From 2009 through 2014, a total of 224 new elements have been added to the list. As of the writing of this essay in early 2015, the list contains 314 elements.[10]

Case Studies

While folklorists have long been involved in UNESCO and ICH initiatives, working with people at all levels of policy creation and implementation, scholarship on these subjects is currently expanding exponentially.[11] This is in part because the 2003 Convention forced many of us who had not explicitly studied UNESCO before to recognize how global policies are affecting people and cultural practices in communities where we work. In an informal conversation during the American Folklore Society (AFS) annual meeting in 2011, two of us (Foster and Gilman) compared the way friends and colleagues in our respective research sites (Japan and Malawi) were thinking about ICH issues. This casual exchange led us to organize a formal panel for the 2012 annual meeting focused on disparate local reactions to UNESCO. Participants included the two of us as well as Carol Silverman (Macedonia) and Kyoim Yun (South Korea). The panel was well attended and well received, with lively discussion from audience members who brought different perspectives and experiences to the table, often based on their own research with ICH stakeholders in a wide range of contexts. This enthusiasm drove home the fact that because of our deep and ongoing engagement with particular communities, folklorists are often uniquely positioned to present on-the-ground perspectives for comparative scholarship. For better or for worse, folklorists also often play an influential role within communities grappling with ICH concerns, and it is important to continue to think critically about our own positionality.

Given the enthusiastic reception of our panel presentation at the AFS meeting, we decided to further our initial comparative exploration by producing the current volume. We asked two more scholars, Leah Lowthorp (India) and Ziying You (China), to contribute essays on their research, for a total of six case studies. We then solicited critical commentary from three scholars (Anthony Seeger, Valdimar Tr. Hafstein, and Dorothy Noyes) who have long theorized ICH issues or been directly involved in UNESCO's activities in various capacities. The goal of this volume is to draw on our fieldwork with residents in places affected by (or interested in) UNESCO so that we can present, as much as possible, a variety of esocultural views. In particular, each one of the case studies in this work concerns a local ICH element that either has been recognized by, nominated for, or is being discussed in terms of the 2003 Convention.

I should reiterate here that "heritage regimes" are always multi-layered and entail interaction between global, national, regional, and local entities; as Regina F. Bendix, Aditya Eggert, and Arnika Peselmann (2012b, 12) have clearly demonstrated, the 2003 Convention involved the creation of "corresponding bureaucracies" to deal with the implementation and management of cultural policies. The essays presented in our own collection touch on these layers and the bureaucratic structures through which they interact, but they especially make an effort to focus on local agency—which of course ultimately consists of multiple individual voices. In presenting these studies, we also make no claims of objectivity; all the authors have long been involved with the communities we are writing about, and our own subjectivities cannot be untangled from the voices we showcase. Having said that, however, and further recognizing that the very nature of our project deals with heterogeneous cultural contexts, we have made every effort to prepare these essays for productive comparative and contrastive analyses.

Specifically, we have kept each essay short and asked contributors to adhere to the same basic guidelines in structuring their studies. Each essay begins with (1) a paragraph briefly introducing the ICH element under consideration, followed by (2) a description of the location of the ICH element under consideration, with geographical, national, regional, ethnic, demographic, economic, touristic, or other relevant information. Next the author (3) introduces and describes the *when, where, why, who,* and *how* of the particular ICH element and (4) its current status with regard to UNESCO—including whether it has been inscribed on the Representative List or is only being discussed on a regional or national level. Each author also provides insight into (5) the on-the-ground perspectives, exploring local discourses about UNESCO and ICH and considering questions such as: What does "UNESCO" signify to the communities involved? What does it mean to be inscribed, or not inscribed, on the Representative List? Does it affect people economically or in other ways? How are words like *ICH* or *UNESCO* interpreted within local languages and vernacular discourses? Finally, each essay concludes with (6) a discussion in which the author contextualizes local discourses theoretically or historically or speculates about the future of the element or the communities in question.

These are the general parameters for the essays that follow, yet the particularities intrinsic to each research site inevitably produce diverse foci and a different balance of information. But of course, this is one objective of the collection in the first place—to highlight the impossibility of a one-size-fits-all template for heritage and to emphasize the diversity of reactions and local effects of UNESCO decisions. Our essays are by no means unique in their focus on particular communities and grassroots responses—folklorists, anthropologists, and other scholars have long produced excellent ethnographic studies of groups of all sizes around the world grappling with ICH issues.[12] However, by presenting relatively formulaic case studies in close juxtaposition, our collection offers carefully rendered snapshots of diverse places at a particular moment and provides a unique opportunity for productive comparison. In a gesture toward what Dorothy Noyes (2008, 41) has eloquently labeled *humble theory,* "we begin to think in the act of describing and see particulars in the act of comparing."

Indeed, even as each case study brings forth issues that are most relevant to people in the community in question, the three discussions that follow draw on these specifics to expand the conversation, seeking commonalities and differences and examining what these particular examples, when placed in conversation with each other, reveal about the broader context. Our three discussants bring diverse experiences and perspectives to ICH processes. As President and later Secretary General of the International Council of Traditional Music (ICTM), Anthony Seeger served as the liaison between ICTM and UNESCO and was editor of the ICTM/UNESCO CD series. As ICTM Secretary General, he was in charge of coordinating the scientific and technical evaluations of the 2003 and 2005 Masterpieces nominations, which gave him direct experience with multiple stages in the nomination and review processes. Valdimar Tr. Hafstein was a participant-observer in UNESCO's expert committee that drafted the ICH Convention in 2003. He also served as head of the Icelandic delegation to the first meeting of the Intergovernmental Committee for the Safeguarding of the Intangible Cultural Heritage in 2006, and he chaired the Icelandic UNESCO Commission from 2011 to 2012. He has additionally acted as a consultant to the Swedish and Norwegian governments on the implementation of the ICH Convention. Folklorist Dorothy Noyes became interested in UNESCO and ICH when the Patum, a fire festival in the Catalan region of Spain that has been the major focus of her fieldwork, received a UNESCO Masterpiece designation. She has published several important articles on this process, both in terms of practice and theory, and is currently a Fellow of the Göttingen Interdisciplinary Research Group in Cultural Property.

A number of the key questions and themes that emerge across the case studies and the commentaries include issues of terminology, power struggles between local, national, and international stakeholders, the effects of tourism and commodification on local communities and cultural practices, the value of international recognition, and the implications of selectivity. Ultimately, what becomes evident throughout this volume is that in some places a UNESCO designation is seen as a financial boon, in some places it is a point of pride and identity, in some places it is a burden, and elsewhere it is merely an adornment or, for that matter, not even on the radar screen. By exploring this diversity of understandings of ICH, our collection of essays will hopefully prove greater than the sum of its parts. Ideally, as a multi-authored, multi-sited ethnography of local engagements with global decisions, it provides a glimpse into emerging interpretations of what culture is, what it does, and what it may become.

Acknowledgments

First and foremost, on behalf of Lisa Gilman and myself, I thank Jason Baird Jackson for managing the peer review process for this book in its initial form as a special issue of the *Journal of Folklore Research*. This allowed me, as editor of *JFR*, to serve with no conflict of interest as guest coeditor and contributing author. We also give our immense thanks to two anonymous reviewers who generously read the manuscript and provided invaluable feedback on individual essays and the work as a whole. Gary Dunham and Michael Regoli of Indiana University Press enthusiastically supported the idea of transforming the special issue into a book, and Steve Stanzak worked tirelessly to make it happen, managing the editing process and even creating the index. Our sincere gratitude also goes to Chad Buterbaugh and Emmie Pappa Eddy for their patient copyediting. Although I wrote this introductory essay and take full responsibility for any errors or omissions herein, it was through constant exchange and discussion with Lisa Gilman that it came together. Despite the fact that during much of this project she was in Malawi and I was in Japan—and the other authors were scattered around the globe—this book is truly a collaborative effort.

Notes

1. *Intangible cultural heritage* is a "technical, somewhat awkward term" (Kurin 2004, 67) but in recent years it seems to have become the generally accepted umbrella expression. Of course, the Standard English term and its "official" French (*patrimoine culturel immatériel*) and Spanish language (*patrimonio cultural inmaterial*) equivalents are translated differently into different languages, where they can take on starkly diverse shades and nuances. For discussions of UNESCO's terminology and definitions, see Kirshenblatt-Gimblett 2006 and the essays in Smith and Akagawa 2009, most explicitly Aikawa-Faure 2009.

2. For a recent exploration of these concerns, see for example the special issue of *Gradhiva* (Berliner and Bortolotto 2013).

3. For an exploration of *community* and related terms, see Noyes 2003; in terms of ICH, see Noyes 2006 and Blake 2009.

4. Moreover, as Chiara De Cesari (2012, 408) puts it, "What is also peculiar about the international heritage regime in relation to its impact on 'local communities' is a paradox, namely, that the former both empowers and disempowers the latter."

5. Research into heritage issues is also deeply connected with the study of tourism and other fields in which folklorists and anthropologists have contributed valuable insights and comparative perspectives. Seminal works on these connections include, but are certainly not limited to, Kirshenblatt-Gimblett 1998 and Bruner 2005.

6. "International Conventions are subject to ratification, acceptance or accession by States. They define rules with which the States undertake to comply." See "General introduction to the standard-setting instruments of UNESCO" at http://portal.unesco.org/en/ev.php-URL_ID=23772&URL_DO=DO_TOPIC&URL_SECTION=201.html.

7. For text of the Convention, see UNESCO 2003.

8. The clause of the Convention establishing the list reads: "In order to ensure better visibility of the intangible cultural heritage and awareness of its significance, and to encourage dialogue which respects cultural diversity, the Committee, upon the proposal of the States Parties concerned, shall establish, keep up to date and publish a Representative List of the Intangible Cultural Heritage of Humanity" (Article 16[1]). There is also a "List of Intangible Cultural Heritage in Need of Urgent Safeguarding," but it was the Representative List that was the most contentious and ultimately represents "a compromise solution reached after intense confrontations between national delegates who wanted to create a merit-based 'List of Treasures' or 'List of Masterpieces' similar to the World Heritage List, those who would rather have seen an inclusive universal inventory of traditional practices, and those who wanted no list at all" (Hafstein 2009, 93).

9. For the Masterpiece criteria, see UNESCO 2000. For more on the development, context, and review process, see Nas 2002; Kirshenblatt-Gimblett 2004, 2006; Kurin 2004; Aikawa 2004; Seeger 2009.

10. View the UNESCO lists of intangible cultural heritage and register of best safeguarding practices at http://www.unesco.org/culture/ich/index.php?lg=en&pg=00559.

11. Such scholarship is arguably more advanced in Europe and Asia, but both ICH and UNESCO are increasingly becoming keywords for scholars in North America as well. The theme of the 2007 Joint Annual Meeting held by the American Folklore Society and the Folklore Studies Association of Canada was "The Politics and Practices of Intangible Cultural Heritage." Over the last several years, I have also noticed a marked increase in the number of folklore and ethnomusicology graduate students at Indiana University interested in researching such issues.

12. Along with folklore and anthropology publications, valuable case studies and close readings of local situations can be found in journals explicitly focusing on heritage issues, such as the *International Journal of Heritage Studies* and the *International Journal of Intangible Heritage*, as well as related venues such as *Museum International, Annals of Tourism Research,* and others.

References Cited

Aikawa, Noriko. 2004. "An Historical Overview of the Preparation of the UNESCO International Convention for the Safeguarding of the Intangible Cultural Heritage." *Museum International* 56 (1–2): 137–49.

Aikawa-Faure, Noriko. 2009. "From the Proclamation of Masterpieces to the *Convention for the Safeguarding of Intangible Cultural Heritage.*" In *Intangible*

Heritage, edited by Laurajane Smith and Natsuko Akagawa, 13–44. New York: Routledge.

Bendix, Regina F., Aditya Eggert, and Arnika Peselmann, eds. 2012a. *Heritage Regimes and the State*. Göttingen: Universitätsverlag Göttingen.

———. 2012b. "Introduction: Heritage Regimes and the State." In *Heritage Regimes and the State*, edited by Regina F. Bendix, Aditya Eggert, and Arnika Peselmann, 11–20. Göttingen: Universitätsverlag Göttingen.

Berliner, David, and Chiara Bortolotto, eds. 2013. "Le monde selon l'Unesco." Special issue. *Gradhiva* 18.

Blake, Janet. 2009. "UNESCO's 2003 *Convention on Intangible Cultural Heritage*: The Implications of Community Involvement in 'Safeguarding.'" In *Intangible Heritage*, edited by Laurajane Smith and Natsuko Akagawa, 45–73. New York: Routledge.

Bruner, Edward M. 2005. *Culture on Tour: Ethnographies of Travel*. Chicago: University of Chicago Press.

De Cesari, Chiara. 2012. "Thinking through Heritage Regimes." In *Heritage Regimes and the State*, edited by Regina F. Bendix, Aditya Eggert, and Arnika Peselmann, 399–413. Göttingen: Universitätsverlag Göttingen.

Di Giovine, Michael A. 2009. *The Heritage-Scape: UNESCO, World Heritage, and Tourism*. Lanham, MD. Rowman and Littlefield.

Hafstein, Valdimar Tr. 2009. "Intangible Heritage as a List: From the Masterpieces to Representation." In *Intangible Heritage*, edited by Laurajane Smith and Natsuko Akagawa, 93–111. New York: Routledge.

Kirshenblatt-Gimblett, Barbara. 1998. *Destination Culture: Tourism, Museums, and Heritage*. Berkeley: University of California Press.

———. 2004. "Intangible Heritage as Metacultural Production." *Museum International* 56 (1–2): 52–65.

———. 2006. "World Heritage and Cultural Economics." In *Museum Frictions: Public Cultures/Global Transformations*, edited by Ivan Karp, Corinne A. Kratz, Lynn Szwaja, and Tomás Ybarra-Frausto, 161–201. Durham, NC: Duke University Press.

Kurin, Richard. 2004. "Safeguarding Intangible Cultural Heritage in the 2003 UNESCO Convention: A Critical Appraisal." *Museum International* 56 (1–2): 66–77.

Kuutma, Kristin. 2012. "Between Arbitration and Engineering: Concepts and Contingencies in the Shaping of Heritage Regimes." In *Heritage Regimes and the State*, edited by Regina F. Bendix, Aditya Eggert, and Arnika Peselmann, 21–38. Göttingen: Universitätsverlag Göttingen.

Matsuura, Koïchiro. 2007. "28th Session of the World Heritage Committee (Suzhou, 28 June 2004)." In *New Ignorances, New Literacies: Selected Speeches 2003–2004*, 177–80. Paris: UNESCO.

Miyata Shigeyuki. 2007. "Mukei bunka isan hogo ni okeru kokusaiteki wakugumi keisei" [Formation of an international framework for the protection of intangible cultural heritage]. *Mukei bunka isan kenkyū hōkoku* 1:1–24.

Nas, Peter J. M. 2002. "Masterpieces of Oral and Intangible Culture: Reflections on the World Heritage List." *Cultural Anthropology* 43 (1): 139–48.

Noyes, Dorothy. 2003. "Group." In *Eight Words for the Study of Expressive Culture*, edited by Burt Feintuch, 7–41. Urbana: University of Illinois Press.

———. 2006. "The Judgment of Solomon: Global Protections for Tradition and the Problem of Community Ownership." *Cultural Analysis* 5:27–56.

———. 2008. "Humble Theory." *Journal of Folklore Research* 45 (1): 37–43.

Sano, Mayuko. 2005. "International Recognition and the Future of Traditional Culture: A View from and toward UNESCO." In *Traditional Japanese Arts and Crafts in the 21st Century: Reconsidering the Future from an International Perspective*, edited by Inaga Shigemi and Patricia Fister, 365–85. Kyoto: International Research Center for Japanese Studies.

Seeger, Anthony. 2009. "Lessons Learned from the ICTM (NGO) Evaluation of Nominations for the UNESCO *Masterpieces of the Oral and Intangible Heritage of Humanity*, 2001–5." In *Intangible Heritage*, edited by Laurajane Smith and Natsuko Akagawa, 112–28. New York: Routledge.

Smith, Laurajane, and Natsuko Akagawa, eds. 2009. *Intangible Heritage*. New York: Routledge.

UNESCO. 2000. Proclamation of Masterpieces of the Oral and Intangible Heritage of Humanity. Reference CL/3553. April 26. Paris: UNESCO. http://unesdoc .unesco.org/images/0015/001541/154155E.pdf.

———. 2001. *Proclamation of Masterpieces of the Oral and Intangible Heritage of Humanity: Guide for the Presentation of Candidature Files*. Paris: UNESCO. http:// unesdoc.unesco.org/images/0012/001246/124628eo.pdf.

———. 2003. Convention for the Safeguarding of the Intangible Cultural Heritage. MISC/2003/CLT/CH/14. October 17. Paris: UNESCO. http://unesdoc .unesco.org/images/0013/001325/132540e.pdf.

———. 2009. "Evaluation of the Nominations for Inscription on the Representative List of the Intangible Cultural Heritage of Humanity." Convention for the Safeguarding of the Intangible Cultural Heritage: Intergovernmental Committee for the Safeguarding of the Intangible Cultural Heritage. Fourth session, Abu Dhabi, United Arab Emirates. ITH/09/4.COM/CONF.209/13. 28 September to 2 October. Paris: UNESCO. http://www.unesco.org/culture /ich/doc/src/ITH-09-4.COM-CONF.209-13-Rev.2-EN.pdf.

MICHAEL DYLAN FOSTER is Associate Professor of Folklore and East Asian Studies at Indiana University. He is the author of *Pandemonium and Parade: Japanese Monsters and the Culture of Yōkai* (2009), *The Book of Yōkai: Mysterious Creatures of Japanese Folklore* (2015), and numerous articles on Japanese folklore, literature, and media.

Local Studies

1   Voices on the Ground: Kutiyattam, UNESCO, and the Heritage of Humanity

KUTIYATTAM SANSKRIT THEATER of Kerala state was recognized as India's first UNESCO Masterpiece of the Oral and Intangible Heritage of Humanity in 2001. Looking back a decade later, how has UNESCO recognition impacted both the art and the lives of its artists? Based upon two years of ethnographic research from 2008 to 2010 among Kutiyattam artists in Kerala, India, this essay follows the art's postrecognition trajectory through its increasing mediatization, institutionalization, and liberalization. Drawing on extended interviews with over fifty Kutiyattam actors, actresses, and drummers, it focuses on reclaiming the voices of affected artists on the ground.

Location: Kerala, India

Kerala is a state largely characterized by exceptionalism. Located on the southwestern coast of the Indian subcontinent along the Arabian Sea (figure 1), the region was known historically for its spice trade with much of the ancient world. At the turn of the twentieth century, Kerala was known for a number of exceptional characteristics—a matrilineal kinship system that gave women comparatively greater autonomy than women in other areas of India; the rule of distance pollution that created the most rigid caste system in India, with lower caste groups not only "untouchable" but "unapproachable" as well; and the relative religious equality, in terms of both tolerance and sheer numbers, between its resident Hindu, Christian, Muslim, and Jewish populations.[1] In the course of the twentieth century, Kerala experienced what Robin Jeffrey (1992, 2) has termed "a social collapse more complete than anywhere in India" that entailed the destruction of the matrilineal inheritance system, the spread of formal education and associated rising political

17

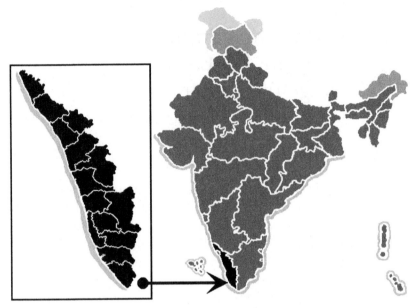

FIGURE 1
Map of Kerala. Public domain image by Saravask, Wikimedia Commons.
http://commons.wikimedia.org/wiki/File:India_map_kerala.png.

activism, and an increasing cash economy that sparked land redistribution legislation by the world's first (1957) democratically elected Communist government.[2]

The discourse of Kerala's exceptionalism is most often articulated through what has become known as the Kerala model of development. Formulated in a 1975 report for the United Nations, the model is characterized by Kerala's low per capita income and high levels of unemployment and poverty coupled with indicators more typical of highly industrialized regions of the developed world, including high levels of literacy and life expectancy and low levels of fertility and infant and maternal mortality (CDS 1975).[3] Kerala currently has the highest literacy rate in India (93.91 percent), lowest infant mortality rate (1.4 percent), lowest population growth (4.86 percent), and only natural sex ratio (1.087:1 women-to-men)—factors that have often been attributed to the state's dominant matrilineal past and political mobilization of social rights led by Kerala's main Communist party, the Communist Party of India (Marxist) (Lukose 2009; see also Jeffrey 1992; Franke and Chasin 1992).[4] More recently acknowledged for its vital role in the propagation of the Kerala model is the state's long-standing migration to Gulf countries.[5] Resulting remittances flowing into the state coupled with India's widespread economic liberalization have led to an expansive commodity culture that gives Kerala, despite continued low economic growth, the highest per capita consumer expenditure in India (Lukose 2009; Kannan and Hari 2002). As the Kerala model has become increasingly unsustainable, however, many have come to regard it as a failed project, a utopia-cum-dystopia characterized by "corruption, moral laxity, stagnant economy, widespread unemployment, high suicide rates, alcoholism, indebtedness, increasing violence against women and, more recently, AIDS" (Sreekumar 2007, 43).[6]

In another manifestation of its discourse of exceptionalism, Kerala has a wider reputation within India as a region preserving "marginal survivals" of an ancient, Sanskritic culture that once spanned the subcontinent.[7] Unlike many other regions of India, most of Kerala was never directly ruled by any foreign power, contributing to its status as a "repository of ancient Sanskrit texts" and cultural forms such as Kutiyattam and Vedic chanting (Raja 2001, xii).[8] The 1909 "discovery" of the Trivandrum Bhasa plays, which first brought Kutiyattam to wider public attention, exemplified Kerala's status as a repository in two ways (Unni 2001).[9] First, the palm leaf manuscripts represented a rediscovery of the famed second-century CE playwright Bhasa, whose plays were thought to have been lost. Second, the wider discovery of Kutiyattam as a living example of Sanskrit drama in performance challenged the long-held assumption that Sanskrit drama was a purely literary form (Sastri 1915; Keith [1924] 1970). This early framing of Kutiyattam as the only living link with ancient Sanskrit theater practice has persisted through the present-day, resulting in an ongoing temporalization of the art in terms of the past.

ICH Element: Kutiyattam Sanskrit Theater

Kutiyattam is often described as the oldest continuously performed theater in the world, with the earliest records documenting the form dated to the tenth century CE.[10] While some have speculated that it began as a secular performance in royal courts, it was definitively incorporated into Kerala's caste-based temple complex in the thirteenth or fourteenth century, where it remained until 1949 (Narayanan 2006). As a *kulathozhil*, or hereditary occupation, it was performed in the temple by both men and women of the Chakyar, Nambiar, and Nangiar castes in exchange for land, food, and clothing. Kutiyattam, meaning "combined acting," embodies a mix of Sanskritic tradition and the indigenous cultural landscape of Kerala. The term encompasses a larger performance complex which includes Kutiyattam, the enactment of Sanskrit drama with multiple actors onstage; Nangiar Koothu, the female acting solo; and Chakyar Koothu, the male verbal solo performance.[11] Composed by famous playwrights such as Bhasa, Saktibhadra, and Harsha, the plays staged date from the second to tenth century CE and are performed according to stage manuals passed down as palm leaf manuscripts. The plots generally revolve around the epics the *Ramayana* and the *Mahabharata*, although a few address Buddhist themes. Recognizable by its rich narrative expression through mudra hand gestures, highly emotive facial expressions, stylized movements, and sparse dialogue of chanted Sanskrit, Kutiyattam focuses on the aesthetic elaboration and extension of each moment. Consequently, only one act is ever performed at a time, lasting anywhere from five to forty-one days on the temple stage. On the public stage, where the majority of performances now occur, an act is usually performed on a single night as one edited, three-hour segment.

In the course of the twentieth century, the system that had sustained Kutiyattam as an elite, temple-based occupation for nearly one thousand years crumbled beneath the artists' feet in a dramatic tide of change that swept over Kerala and the emerging Indian nation. The matrilineal, *gurukula*-system educated, land-owning Kutiyattam community was unalterably affected by the destruction of royal patronage, the Communist land redistribution legislation depriving artists of their lands, and state legislation officially destroying matrilineal inheritance.[12] Many members of Kutiyattam families sought other occupations, thus rejecting the existing agrarian order and becoming "agents of modernity in new forms of employment," like so many others in Kerala who came to associate their hereditary occupations with an increasingly distant past (Osella and Osella 2006, 571).

A few progressive members of the community fought to adapt both the art and their lives to survive the changing times, giving rise to a discourse of endangerment and *samrakshanam* (safeguarding) that

FIGURE 2
From left to right: Kalamandalam Reshmi as Sita, Kalamandalam Sivan Nambudiri as Ravana, and Kalamandalam Krishnakumar as Suthan, 2009. Photograph by author.

has persisted in various incarnations through the present day. Actions that were considered unthinkable at the time, such as performing Kutiyattam outside the temple and democratizing its performance community, are now retrospectively narrated as revolutionarily necessary for the survival of the art form. Guru Painkulam Rama Chakyar is credited with taking Kutiyattam out of the temple for the first time in 1949, with teaching the art's first nonhereditary students in 1965, and with implementing a process of aesthetic reinvention of the art at Kerala Kalamandalam, the state performing arts institution.[13] As a result, contemporary Kutiyattam straddles two spheres: the temple and public spheres of performance—the former inhabited by hereditary performers, both professional and nonprofessional, and the latter by professional performers, both hereditary and nonhereditary.[14] Often depicted as an ancient art of the Chakyars in Kerala today, Kutiyattam defies such stereotypes through the diversity of its community members, who assert their subjectivity as contemporary artists practicing a contemporary art.

Current Status with Regard to UNESCO:
India's First Masterpiece of the Oral and Intangible
Heritage of Humanity (2001)

Paris, 1980: The *UNESCO Features* newsletter reported on a Kutiyattam performance staged in the city as part of the art form's first international tour, funded in part by UNESCO's International Fund for the Promotion of Culture (Kinnane 1980).[15] Paris, 1999: While on tour to Paris again, a UNESCO representative came to the performance and encouraged the Kutiyattam troupe members to apply for a new program that UNESCO was launching.[16] Granted UNESCO funds for the application, it was through the effort of the troupe's leader and a few other key individuals, such as internationally renowned film director Adoor Gopalakrishnan, that Kutiyattam's application was submitted to UNESCO by the Indian government as its only candidate that first year.[17] The art's national and international connections thus laid the foundation for its international recognition. When the first Proclamation of Masterpieces of the Oral and Intangible Heritage of Humanity was subsequently announced in 2001, Kutiyattam became India's first expressive tradition to be so recognized by UNESCO, although not without controversy (figure 3).[18]

While the Indian Ministry of Culture began budgeting a small amount for the "preservation and promotion of intangible heritage of humanity" in 2003, Kutiyattam's action plan began to be implemented in 2004 primarily through a UNESCO/Japan-Funds-in-Trust project, which issued 150,000 US dollars to six institutions over a period of three years (Government of India 2003–4, 182; UNESCO 2007).[19] Under the direct oversight of the UNESCO New Delhi regional office, the funds were used to support meetings of a Kutiyattam network, the revival of plays, publications, student training, public awareness-raising workshops and performances, academic seminars, the production of ten documentaries, and a workshop on basic conservation techniques for palm leaf manuscripts. In 2006, a special fifty-million rupee provision was made in the National Budget for India's three UNESCO Masterpieces—Kutiyattam (2001), Vedic Chanting (2003), and Ramlila (2005).[20] This sparked a fight between two major national institutions for control of the project, the Sangeet Natak Akademi (SNA) and the Indira Gandhi National Center for the Arts (IGNCA). The SNA eventually emerged victorious based on its long-standing financial support

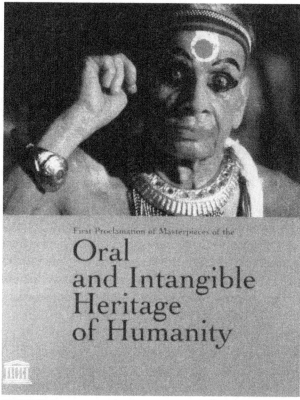

FIGURE 3
Guru Ammannur Madhava Chakyar on the cover of
UNESCO's First Proclamation of Masterpieces of the Oral
and Intangible Heritage of Humanity, 2001. UNESCO.

of Kutiyattam, and in 2007 it founded a national center, Kutiyattam
Kendra, in Kerala's capital city of Trivandrum.[21]

The Sangeet Natak Akademi, India's national academy for dance,
drama, and music, began translating Kutiyattam into national heritage
early on, clearly valuing the art for its "pastness" through its widespread
characterization as "the only surviving link to the ancient Sanskrit
theater" (SNA 1995; see also Lowthorp 2013b). This is part of a longer
process of Indian nation building that, as Vasudha Dalmia (1997) has
argued, appropriated Orientalist discourse through the "nationalization" of Hindu traditions viewed as legitimized in ancient, Sanskrit
texts. Thus viewing Kutiyattam as a marginal survival of an ancient
Vedic (i.e., Hindu) age, the SNA began showcasing and documenting

the art in the 1960s and incorporated it into a funding scheme targeting endangered art forms in the 1970s. This eventually culminated in a "total care plan" for the preservation of Kutiyattam which provided low, steady levels of funding starting in 1991 (SNA 1991–92).[22] With the 2007 opening of the Kutiyattam Kendra, funding for Kutiyattam was significantly increased and the art became included in a small, elite group of the SNA's permanently funded institutions.[23] Remaining under the purview of the SNA, which continues to characterize the art as both endangered and as India's only living link to ancient Sanskrit theater, Kutiyattam's post-UNESCO project implementation has constituted a continuity of state policy, both in discourse and practice.

Kutiyattam Kendra ushered in a number of initiatives. Prioritizing Kutiyattam's transmission, it began distributing augmented student and teacher stipends to three existing and four new institutions.[24] It funded the only carpenter in Kerala making costumes for Kutiyattam and other Kerala arts.[25] Kutiyattam Kendra made the art's public promotion another priority, funding monthly lecture-demonstrations and performances at universities, schools, cultural institutions, temple trusts, and other organizations across Kerala and, to a lesser extent, India. It began organizing an annual performance festival that brought all of the institutions together, as well as various specialized seminars and workshops throughout the year. In 2008, Kutiyattam was incorporated into the Representative List of the Intangible Cultural Heritage of Humanity as per the terms of UNESCO's 2003 Convention, remaining under state patronage via Kutiyattam Kendra. This study, conducted from 2008 to 2010, represents a perspective approximately one decade after UNESCO recognition.[26]

On-the-Ground Perspectives: Mediatization, Social Status, and the Rise of the Institution

One young artist once described to me his understanding of UNESCO, inquiring, "What is UNESCO exactly? We don't know. UNESCO doesn't do anything directly, so for us artists there is no UNESCO. To our knowledge, it is only the Indian government that is doing something."[27] Along with a few artists who openly admitted to me that they didn't know what UNESCO was or what to expect when it recognized Kutiyattam, the majority of artists viewed UNESCO as a distant international organization whose interventions were indirectly facilitated through national and local bodies. A few had had direct interaction with the organization—the twelve artists who performed at UNESCO's Thirty-First General Conference, for example—but even in those institutions that received direct funding from UNESCO/Japan-Funds-in-Trust, contact was facilitated by their largely nonartist institutional leadership.[28]

There was a wide range of perspectives surrounding the UNESCO project formulation and implementation that reflects the diversity of the contemporary Kutiyattam community. Several artists expressed that they didn't feel they had much of a voice in the process, as it was dominated by local and national nonartist institutional leadership, however well-meaning, with meetings sometimes held in languages they largely did not understand—English and Hindi—when SNA or UNESCO representatives attended. While there was a general consensus that the recognition was a good thing for the art form, opinions varied over exactly to what extent. Some attributed to UNESCO a minimal role, having provided "only money" or "only recognition, like an award." Others ascribed a more pivotal role to the recognition, expressing the view that if not for UNESCO, Kutiyattam "would have died out in ten or twenty years since no one would come to study it." Most artists, however, fell somewhere in between, both recognizing UNESCO's ephemeral role—as one artist put it, "UNESCO is like a rain that comes and goes suddenly, but doesn't stay"—and the lasting impact that its recognition has had upon both Kutiyattam's general social standing and its position vis-à-vis the Indian government. Among the spectrum of sentiments expressed on the issue, those subjects most often raised—the art's increased societal recognition and the rise of the institution to its current monolithic prominence—will be discussed here.

UNESCO's 2001 recognition of Kutiyattam brought a flurry of media attention. As Kerala has both the highest literacy and media exposure rates in India, this attention made a noticeable impact on Kerala's public imagination. When an artist is asked his profession, his reply is no longer met with a blank stare. Kutiyattam's greater media presence has led to increased societal recognition, but it has not translated into greater audiences as many had hoped. As one artist noted: "Kutiyattam spread out superficially, like smoke. People have come to recognize the name and costume but don't come to watch performances." The smoky tendrils of greater Kutiyattam awareness spread

FIGURE 4
Margi Usha performing Nangiar Koothu, 2006. Photograph by author.

throughout Kerala, India, and the world on the winds of UNESCO.
In Kerala, however, the recognition carried the wider misconception
that artists were given a lot of UNESCO money and should thus perform without pay—festival organizers now eager to include Kutiyattam
for its advertising value are often not ready to pay for it. Despite the

overall greater media attention and general interest in the art since UNESCO recognition, more popular art forms like Kathakali and Mohiniyattam, seen as icons of Kerala culture, still dominate Kerala's arts media and wider performance arenas.

The greatest impact this wider social recognition has had is upon the way many artists relate to their art. As one artist poignantly expressed: "The greatest effect was that working artists had an awakening, they found a belief in themselves. That was the *greatest*. Now we're really proud to be in Kutiyattam. It has gained value. When we go to programs we are happy, because everyone doesn't see us as unimportant anymore. They see us and treat us with respect." Several former students of Kerala Kalamandalam painfully recounted past experiences of being made fun of by students of other art forms, who would mock Kutiyattam's singsong method of text recitation and taunt them that they were studying for nothing, that they would never find a job. Narrating the stark juxtaposition of the recent past, they explained: "But nowadays this doesn't happen. Our respect grew."

The effect of UNESCO recognition most often noted by artists was their newfound ability to make a living as Kutiyattam performers due to an increase in institutions and funding, indicative of a post-recognition rise of the institution. With institutionalization a means of becoming visible to the state, the art's increased institutionalization further integrated it into existing national structures of heritage and state patronage. As I have argued elsewhere, Kutiyattam's UNESCO recognition thus represented a hyper-nationalization of the art, as it was chosen to represent the cultural face of a national India on a global scale (Lowthorp 2013a, 2013b). The art's postrecognition institutionalization, however, differed from the previous period in one significant way. While earlier institutions were primarily established and run by nonartists with the ability to successfully navigate the structures of state funding, postrecognition institutions were founded and run exclusively by artists, thereby disrupting existing structures of authority and giving artists greater self-determination.[29]

Nearly all artists agreed that the Indian government founded the Kutiyattam Kendra and increased the art's funding levels as a direct result of its UNESCO recognition. This was unanimously viewed as a positive aspect of a complex issue that has both positive and negative ramifications for the art. With the 2007 establishment of Kutiyattam Kendra, many artists received a stable, living wage for the first time in their lives. The number of institutions receiving SNA grants more than doubled, adding a large number of artists to the ranks of what is considered "normal" wage earners in Kerala.[30] This increase in funding has consequently had a profound effect upon the artists and their lives. While providing peace of mind and the increased confidence that comes with a steady income, it has also contributed to increased social status, greater social mobility, and improved marriageability of young male artists. Although many young male artists hoping to marry were previously forced to abandon their art for more profitable employment in the Gulf countries, the situation has now changed. As one artist reflected: "Support for performance came, standards came, and identity and power came with it. Kutiyattam became a profession with a salary base. After getting a salary here, Ramesh was able to marry, because he could say he works here. That's a real social change."[31] This change has also given the current generation of students, already encouraged by the introduction of a generous stipend, greater confidence in the art and hope that they too may one day be able to make their "life's path" (*jivitha margam*) through Kutiyattam.

As noted earlier, the effect that UNESCO recognition has had upon Kutiyattam is viewed as a complex issue with both positive and negative aspects. One of the main critiques artists made of recognition concerned the unequal access to and distribution of funding. Kutiyattam Kendra's current funding model privileges institutional seniority over artistic seniority, with senior institutions receiving much higher grants and income allotments for individual artists than those of junior institutions. Consequently, junior artists employed at senior institutions are paid nearly twice as much as more experienced artists at junior institutions, a situation nearly everyone finds unjust. Additionally, although Kutiyattam has been undergoing a process of institutionalization since the 1960s, within most previous funding structures there had been room for independent artists. In contrast, the UNESCO/Japan-Funds-In-Trust project was implemented solely through institutions and left many with the feeling that it was mostly the well-known artists within them that benefitted, excluding both non-institutionally affiliated artists and lesser known artists within those institutions.[32] Furthermore, with Kutiyattam Kendra, the SNA introduced an institution-centric model that left no room for its previous funding of both independent artists and Kerala Kalamandalam. Given the small total number of Kutiyattam artists, many were disappointed to see that, as they phrased it, "only institutions benefitted." As one artist asserted, "If UNESCO wanted to save Kutiyattam, it should have saved everyone, not just certain people."[33]

There was also a widespread sentiment that with the increase in funding, both devotion to and quality of the art have decreased. This was expressed partly through generational difference in comments such as "this new generation uses the art for living; they aren't living for the art." This sentiment encapsulates two fears: the fear of privileging the pursuit of money and fame over the art and the fear of artistic stagnation through financial security. While the latter was more generally portrayed as a danger to be avoided in the future, the former was often expressed through a discussion of the postrecognition explosion of new choreographies. As one young artist explained: "You can't only do the old pieces, because the world we are seeing is new, so an actor has to do new things. If there hadn't been experiments like that in the past, Kutiyattam wouldn't exist today." While artists view innovation as a vital constituent of an ever-changing art, most assert it should ultimately be made for the greater good of the art while maintaining its "frame." The majority of earlier choreographic innovation had been undertaken by senior gurus and tended to constitute revivals of group pieces previously existing in Kutiyattam's repertoire. While these types of choreographies have continued, the current trend is characterized by the prevalence of new, solo pieces many artists consider inspired by government funding initiatives. Composed by all levels of artists, they are generally accompanied by a sense of personal ownership, competition, and ephemerality, performed expressly by their composers usually only a few times in total. In contrast with the standard repertoire, which tends to be collaborative and is performed by everyone again and again, the newer choreographies are viewed by many as motivated by the pursuit of money and personal fame rather than the greater good of Kutiyattam.

The final critique discussed here centers around the appropriateness of an institutional model for Kutiyattam. Albeit already widely institutionalized, the establishment of an institution-centric Kutiyattam Kendra and the stricter regulations that came with it brought this issue into greater focus for many artists. While the previous model left day-to-day practices largely unregulated, artists became required to reside at their institution six days per week, to formally request time off thereby reducing their salary, to take attendance for both students and artists, and to submit paperwork detailing their monthly activities.

While salaries were viewed positively by everyone and regulations considered necessary to a certain degree, this overall process was perceived by many as a loss of freedom.[34] One artist reflected: "We were totally free with our programs but now that has all been regulated. Now we have a condition of normal working people. It is good for an office but bad for art." The idea that art requires flexibility and freedom to develop was fundamentally shared by artists, who continue to hold up the unregulated gurukula model as the ideal environment for Kutiyattam. As one artist described in rich metaphor: "If we put a plant in our garden and restrain it in a strict way, it won't develop. But if we take it to the forest, it will develop into a majestic tree. Artists need a forest atmosphere, not a garden atmosphere. An institution is like a garden . . . but a forest is natural. The best development for Kutiyattam is always a natural development."

Discussion: Liberalization, State Patronage, and Dynamic Safeguarding

The range of artists' reactions to UNESCO recognition and its legacy largely evidences tensions surrounding a liberalizing Kutiyattam. *Liberalization* as a term is generally preferred to *globalization* in the Indian context to describe both the opening of its economy in the 1990s to global market forces and the profound impact this had upon its political, economic, and cultural landscapes.[35] In Kerala, intense economic liberalization and heightened levels of nonelite Gulf migration have led to conspicuous consumption practices that assume key roles in social distinction and identity fashioning through the present day (Osella and Osella 2003). Comments about young artists using the art to live rather than living for the art index an Indian generation known as "liberalization's children," characterized as technology savvy, admiring capitalism, desiring wealth, preferring jobs in the private sector, and consuming guiltlessly (Lukose 2009). Prior to UNESCO recognition, the act of choosing Kutiyattam as a profession clearly signified artistic dedication, as it meant rejecting more profitable employment.[36] But now that Kutiyattam has become an avenue for artists to make a decent living, albeit still meager, these boundaries have become blurred. Many artists were steadfast in their assertion that "if you start thinking about money, Kutiyattam will be lost. You need money to live, but you can't live for money."

FIGURE 5
Ammannur Kuttan Chakyar as Bali, 2009. Photograph by author.

The view that money is necessary to survive but artists shouldn't pursue it was thus complicated by the introduction of salaries, the rise in demand for performances, and the art's increased social status following UNESCO recognition. While everyone genuinely viewed these as positive developments, an underlying aversion toward art as commodity persisted, manifesting in fears about the future and a rising mistrust of the motivations behind both younger artists and the proliferation of new choreographies. As one artist insisted, however, Kutiyattam still represents the choice of artistic dedication and market eschewal: "If a boy is not intelligent, he cannot study Kutiyattam, because he has to remember so many things, he has to study the grammar of *both* Malayalam and Sanskrit. If he is that intelligent, he can go to study BTech or CA and earn three or four times as much."[37] This artist argued that while the basic economic level of Kutiyattam had increased, in light of the changing demands of the surrounding society, the scale of what artists gave up for the art had actually remained the same.

In what might seem like a contradiction, despite fears that Kutiyattam's greater social and economic success signals its impending surrender to the market economy, artists fundamentally agree that

Kutiyattam needs patronage to survive. Statements such as "art needs patronage" and "a Kutiyattam artist cannot make a living only through performance, since it has never been that kind of commercial art," place the art squarely *outside* of a neoliberal frame that "seeks to bring all human action into the domain of the market" (Harvey 2005, 3). With the founding of the SNA in 1953, the newly established Indian government explicitly acknowledged its responsibility of "filling the vacuum" left by crumbled systems of royal arts patronage. Heralding a "new awakening and cultural resurgence . . . to take place in the country under a new system of patronage hitherto unknown to Indian Arts," this approach has been maintained despite its conflict with the nation's wider liberalization policies (SNA 1953–58). While the SNA provided low levels of funding to Kutiyattam over the years, its opening of Kutiyattam Kendra symbolized a guarantee that the art would be patronized indefinitely, albeit via a controlled institutional form. The coupling of the acknowledgment that Kutiyattam cannot survive in the marketplace with the assertion that it will, indeed, survive through state patronage, represents a mode of resistance to market tyranny that continues to value the economically unsustainable as a public good (Bourdieu 1998). Through its ICH program, UNESCO, a champion of modernity, frames postmodernity as the enemy in its struggle against a globalization (i.e., neoliberalism) seen to threaten global cultural diversity.[38] As evident in the Masterpieces program, which expressly recognized arts that "risk disappearing" and framed tourism, often one of the only options for economic sustainability, as a threat, UNESCO vilified the cultural commodification feared by Kutiyattam artists as a result of recognition (UNESCO 2001). It simultaneously idealized a model that the Indian state had long followed and simply intensified for Kutiyattam postrecognition, that of the state as patron-ad-infinitum. It raises the question of whether this economically unsustainable model, that of the state as patron, is the only acceptable path forward offered by UNESCO within the boundaries of its modernist limits.

This concept of infinite patronage was also deeply implicated in the way artists conceived of the concept of "safeguarding" (*samrakshanam*), namely as the financial support of artists. This was evidenced through queries such as, "Without safeguarding the artists how will you safeguard the art?"[39] This equation of safeguarding with steady patronage framed artists' concerns for the future, particularly for the next generation: "Our generation has been safeguarded, but what about the future generation? When our students finish, where will they work? Will they be able to continue in the art?"[40] As a process facilitating the continuity of artists rather than a strictly defined form, this is a dynamic safeguarding based on a concept of art as inherently changing and adapting to contemporary audiences. I have described this elsewhere as "dynamic" or "fluid authenticity," namely the reflexive recognition, as in the words of one senior guru, that "art will never disappear, but the shape of its performance, what persists, will continually change" (Lowthorp 2013a). Tied to assertions made by several artists that "Kutiyattam is not a museum piece," this perspective was institutionalized in the very founding of the SNA, inaugurated with the words: "Nowhere is it truer than in the field of art that to sustain means to create. Traditions cannot be preserved but can only be created afresh" (SNA 1953–58).

UNESCO's definition of intangible cultural heritage as "constantly recreated" resonates with the conception of Kutiyattam artists and the Indian arts establishment of art as ever-changing (UNESCO 2003, 2). The ICH program was developed to counter a hegemonic Western heritage discourse that privileges material forms and assumes safeguarding to be a static process, one that locates "authenticity" in urforms rather than in the moment of change itself.[41] While the program offers dynamic safeguarding (i.e., acknowledging cultural change) as a "new" tool, UNESCO's toolbox itself has remained the same. Forged by the European Enlightenment, it replays "the oldest modernist angst, 'the specter of difference vanishing'" (Comaroff and Comaroff 2009, 23; cf. Bayart 2005).[42] It refashions the "saved-from-the-fire" narrative of salvage anthropology and folkloristics, pitting "endangered" culture against a new enemy—globalization (Abrahams 1993; see also Hafstein 2004). From a discursive perspective, the UNESCO ICH program is, indeed, "caught between freezing the practice and addressing the inherently processual nature of culture" (Kirshenblatt-Gimblett 2004, 58–59). UNESCO's modernist toolbox is thus filled with both static and dynamic safeguarding tools to be employed at the discretion of each nation-state, making it essential to examine the processes whereby this toolbox is differentially utilized, and differentially affects constituent communities, around the world.[43]

Acknowledgments

I would like to thank the Kutiyattam community for generously welcoming me into their lives and allowing me to represent their voices in wider arenas. Research and writing for this essay were funded by a 2008–09 William Penn Fellowship from the University of Pennsylvania in conjunction with the Philadelphia Folksong Society, a 2009 Kenneth Goldstein Summer Research Award from the Graduate Program in Folklore and Folklife at the University of Pennsylvania, a 2009–10 American Institute of Indian Studies Junior Fellowship, and a 2010–11 Zwicker Memorial Fund Dissertation Award from the Department of Anthropology at the University of Pennsylvania.

Notes

1. I am careful not to follow the trend of romanticizing the status of women in Kerala's matrilineal-yet-patriarchal history. The relative autonomy of women in Kerala must be considered in light of the fact that the British had already legislated away much of women's autonomy in other areas of India (Sangari and Vaid 1989).

2. The world's first truly democratically elected Communist government was in the tiny Italian city-state of San Marino in 1945, though scholars often sideline this in favor of Kerala's claim.

3. See also Lukose 2009 and Parayil 2000. The Kerala model was significant because it belied previous assumptions that increased GDP was the only avenue of development.

4. Demographic data is drawn from the 2011 census conducted by the Government of India, Ministry of Home Affairs (http://censusindia.gov.in/). Other factors cited for these statistics are the enlightened policies of the monarchs of Travancore and Cochin princely states, the intervention of Christian missionaries in areas of education and health, and caste reform movements (Sreekumar 2007).

5. Beginning with the 1970s oil boom, this migration has been largely nonelite and male. Zachariah, Prakash, and Irudaya (2002) argue that increased numbers of educated youth and lack of employment opportunities sparked the high rates of migration, which in turn have surpassed the Kerala model in alleviating poverty. See also Lukose 2009.

6. Lukose (2009) and Thomas (2011) have argued against Kerala's exceptionalism for similar reasons.

7. The concept of marginal survival is part of the Finnish or comparative method in folkloristics and encompasses the idea that traditions often survive on the periphery, away from the center in which they may have originated but no longer exist.

8. Kerala was never ruled by a foreign power with the exception of its Malabar region, which was conquered both by Hyder Ali of Mysore and subsequently by the British, becoming part of the Madras Presidency until Indian independence. See Byrski 1967 for a discussion of Kerala's contribution to the preservation of rare Sanskrit dramatic manuscripts.

9. There is still debate surrounding the authorship of the manuscripts, as argued in Brückner 1999–2000.

10. The record cites King Kulasekhara, ruler of a central Kerala kingdom in the tenth century, as having reformed Kutiyattam and authored the plays *Subhadra Dhananjayam* and *Tapatisamvaranam* (Raja 1974).

11. As *koothu* means dance or performance, Nangiar Koothu and Chakyar Koothu thus mean performance of the Nangiar and Chakyar castes respectively. For an analysis of the history and performance of Nangiar Koothu, see Moser 2008. For that of Kutiyattam, see Gopalakrishnan 2011a, Johan 2014, and Sowle 1982.

12. The gurukula system constitutes a mode of informal education whereby the disciple lives with or near the guru and learns from him within the course of daily life.

13. I approach aesthetics via Mascia-Lees (2011), who crystallizes Merleau-Ponty's (1964, 7) formulation of the aesthetic as a form of embodied knowing in her conception of "aesthetic embodiment," or a "somatically grounded, culturally mediated, affective encounter with the beautiful."

14. In Kerala's conservative temple culture, the temple sphere of performance is still closed to nonhereditary performers of Kutiyattam.

15. Milena Salvini of Mandapa, Paris, in collaboration with Dr. Krysztof Byrski of Poland, organized the 1980 tour of Kerala Kalamandalam's Kutiyattam troupe. Mandapa received funding from UNESCO for various projects involving Indian performing arts over the years (Interview with Milena Salvini, July 2011, Paris).

16. This was the Margi Kutiyattam troupe's first international tour, organized by Milena Salvini of Mandapa and led by Dr. Sudha Gopalakrishnan.

17. The candidature file was written by Dr. Sudha Gopalakrishnan of Margi. For an account of the obstacles and contentions encountered during the application process, see Lowthorp 2013a.

18. Kutiyattam's recognition was interpreted by some in the national culture sector to represent the Indian government's ongoing privileging of Sanskritic cultural forms, further confirmed by the 2003 recognition of Vedic Chanting.

19. The institutions included in the project were Margi, Kerala Kalamandalam, Ammannur Chachu Chakyar Smaraka Gurukulam, Padmashri Mani Madhava Chakyar Smaraka Gurukulam, the International Centre for Kutiyattam, and the Center for the Development of Imaging Technology.

20. This was equivalent to approximately one million US dollars, although the budgeted amount was not spent on the art forms that year due to its late approval and the resulting failure to disburse the funds before the government's March 31 fiscal year end. For more details on the UNESCO recognition and implementation process, see Gopalakrishnan 2011b and Lowthorp 2013a.

21. According to documents in the Ministry of Culture's unpublished file on the national implementation of the UNESCO ICH program, the SNA argued for control based on its long-standing project with Kutiyattam, while the IGNCA argued for control based on its long-standing project with Vedic Chanting.

22. Kutiyattam was incorporated into the Promotion and Preservation of Rare Forms of Traditional Performing Arts scheme in 1974 and the National Centres for Specialised Training in Music and Dance scheme in 1991 (SNA 1974–75, 1991–92).

23. The other institutions include Kathak Kendra and the Jawaharlal Nehru Manipuri Dance Academy, with the Sattriya Kendra added in 2008. Unlike these

others, however, Kutiyattam Kendra is not a training institution but a grants-in-aid institution that distributes grants to gurukulams and training institutions.

24. Senior institutions constitute those already funded by SNA at the time of the founding of Kutiyattam Kendra, namely Margi, Ammannur Chachu Chakyar Smaraka Gurukulam, and Padmashri Mani Madhava Chakyar Smaraka Gurukulam, while junior institutions are those brought into the fold of SNA by Kutiyattam Kendra, namely Pothiyil Gurukulam, Nepathya, Painkulam Ramachakyar Smaraka Kalapeedom, and Krishnan Nambiar Mizhavu Kalari. Senior institutions are given higher salaries along with an annual production and materials grant not offered to junior institutions.

25. The Koppa Nirmanakendram institution was funded with student and teacher stipends and a materials grant. As the only carpenter in Kerala with such knowledge, this has resulted in a continuity of knowledge of costume construction techniques for several other Kerala art forms, including Kathakali, as well.

26. See Moser 2011 for further scholarly and artistic viewpoints on UNESCO's recognition of Kutiyattam ten years out.

27. All Malayalam to English translations are by the author.

28. The artists who performed at UNESCO in October 2001 were Ammannur Madhava Chakyar, P.K. Narayanan Nambiar, Kalamandalam Sivan Nambudiri, Kalamandalam Isvaranunni, Margi Sajeev, Margi Usha, Margi Sathi, G. Venu, Kalamandalam Rajeev, Kalamandalam Hariharan, P.K. Unnikrishnan, and Margi Subramanian Potti.

29. A few nonhereditary artists, however, pointed out to me that all of the new institutions were granted to Chakyars, Kutiyattam's male hereditary performers, although these institutions employ both hereditary and nonhereditary artists. One exception is an institution founded by a female hereditary performer with her nonhereditary, musician husband.

30. The "normal" wages were 7,000 rupees monthly (approximately 155 US dollars), which represents the lowest salary at senior institutions and the midrange salary at junior institutions.

31. Ramesh is a pseudonym.

32. There was also a palpable feeling that much of the UNESCO/Japan-Funds-in-Trust funds never reached the artists themselves, spent instead on costly projects like documentaries that artists never had the opportunity to see and the production of scholarly works in English that most artists couldn't read.

33. The Malayalam verb used by the artists, *samrakshikan*, more widely means to save, to rescue, to safeguard, all rolled into one.

34. By salaries I am referring to the teacher stipends provided by Kutiyattam Kendra. While not technically salaries, since they aren't accompanied by the other benefits of salaried work, most of the artists refer to them as such.

35. For wider discussions of these reforms and their effects, see Deshpande 2003, Mazzarella 2003, and Oza 2006.

36. Under the previous agrarian system, money played a minimal role. At that time, becoming a Kutiyattam artist was determined by birth, not by choice, and meant living a comfortable, although not lavish, life.

37. BTech stands for Bachelor's in Technology and CA for Certified Accountant, both coveted degree courses in Kerala.

38. UNESCO's 2003 Convention states that "the processes of globalization and social transformation . . . give rise . . . to grave threats of deterioration, disappearance and destruction of the intangible cultural heritage" (1).

39. The young hereditary artist Ammannur Rajaneesh Chakyar (2011, 9) ends his essay on UNESCO with the quote, "To protect an art form, one must protect the artist first."

40. These concerns form part of a trend that has pervaded Kutiyattam for at least a half century, namely a sense of perpetual endangerment (Lowthorp 2011, 2013a).

41. See Smith 2006 for a detailed discussion of what she terms the "authorized heritage discourse" (AHD). This hegemonic heritage discourse has generally been discussed in terms of its privileging of material forms of heritage rather than for its formulation of static authenticity.

42. Comaroff and Comaroff (2009, 23) are referring here to Adorno's claim of the homogenizing force of the mass media, which they more widely dub "Adorno as farce."

43. The concept of "endangered culture" requiring "safeguarding" is at base a product of European modernity, whether statically or dynamically approached. I have examined this at length in my dissertation, adapting Diana Taylor's (2003) notion of "scenarios" to formulate what I term "scenarios of endangered culture" as a dominant motif in the narrative of modernity that ultimately results in the production of heritage (Lowthorp 2013a).

References Cited

Abrahams, Roger. 1993. "Phantoms of Romantic Nationalism in Folkloristics." *Journal of American Folklore* 106 (419): 3–37.

Bayart, Jean-Francois. 2005. *The Illusion of Cultural Identity*. Translated by Steven Rendall, Janet Roitman, Cynthia Schoch, and Jonathan Derrick. Chicago: University of Chicago Press.

Bourdieu, Pierre. 1998. *Acts of Resistance: Against the Tyranny of the Market*. New York: The New Press.

Brückner, Heidrun. 1999–2000. "Manuscripts and Performance Traditions of the So-Called 'Trivandrum-Plays' Ascribed to Bhasa: A Report on Work in Progress." *Bulletin d'Études Indiennes* 17–18:501–50.

Byrski, Maria Kryzstof. 1967. "Is Kudiyattam a Museumpiece?" *Sangeet Natak* 5:45–54.

CDS (Centre for Development Studies). 1975. *Poverty, Unemployment, and Development Policy: A Case Study of Selected Issues with Reference to Kerala*. New York: United Nations, Department of Economic and Social Affairs.

Chakyar, Ammannur Rajaneesh. 2011. "Kutiyattam: An Overview of Ten Years after the Declaration of UNESCO." In "Kutiyattam: 10 Years after the UNESCO Declaration," edited by Heike Moser. Special issue, *Indian Folklife* 38:9.

Comaroff, Jean, and John L. Comaroff. 2009. *Ethnicity, Inc.* Chicago: University of Chicago Press.

Dalmia, Vasudha. 1997. *The Nationalization of Hindu Traditions: Bhāratendu Hariśchandra and Nineteenth-Century Banaras.* Delhi: Oxford University Press.

Deshpande, Satish. 2003. *Contemporary India: A Sociological View.* New York: Viking.

Franke, Richard, and Barbara Chasin. 1992. *Kerala: Development through Radical Reform.* Delhi: Promilla, in collaboration with the Institute for Food and Development Policy, San Francisco.

Gopalakrishnan, Sudha. 2011a. *Kutiyattam: The Heritage Theater of India.* New Delhi: Niyogi.

———. 2011b. "Kutiyattam: UNESCO Proclamation and the Change in Institutional Model and Patronage." In "Kutiyattam: 10 Years after the UNESCO Declaration," edited by Heike Moser. Special issue, *Indian Folklife* 38:4–8.

Government of India, Ministry of Culture. 2003–4. "Annual Report 2003–2004." Delhi: Government of India.

Hafstein, Valdimar Tr. 2004. "The Making of Intangible Cultural Heritage: Tradition and Authenticity, Community, and Humanity." PhD diss., University of California, Berkeley.

Harvey, David. 2005. *A Brief History of Neoliberalism.* Oxford: Oxford University Press.

Jeffrey, Robin. 1992. *Politics, Women, and Well-Being: How Kerala Became 'a Model.'* London: Macmillan.

Johan, Virginie. 2014. "Du Jeu au Jeu de l'Acteur de Kutiyattam: Ethnoscènology d'un Théâtre Épique." PhD diss., Université Paris 3.

Kannan, K. P., and K. S. Hari. 2002. "Kerala's Gulf Connection: Emigration, Remittances, and Their Macroeconomic Impact, 1972–2000." Trivandrum Centre for Development Studies Working Paper No. 328.

Keith, A. Berriedale. (1924) 1970. *The Sanskrit Drama: In Its Origin, Development, Theory, and Practice.* Oxford: Oxford University Press.

Kinnane, D. 1980. "Ancient Dance Theater Makes First Appearance Outside India." *UNESCO Features* 24:1–3.

Kirshenblatt-Gimblett, Barbara. 2004. "Intangible Heritage as Metacultural Production." *Museum International* 56 (1–2): 52–65.

Lowthorp, Leah. 2011. "'Post-UNESCO' Kutiyattam: Some Methodological Considerations." In "Kutiyattam: 10 Years after the UNESCO Declaration," edited by Heike Moser. Special issue, *Indian Folklife* 38:10–13.

———. 2013a. "Scenarios of Endangered Culture, Shifting Cosmopolitanisms: Kutiyattam and UNESCO Intangible Cultural Heritage in Kerala, India." PhD diss., University of Pennsylvania.

———. 2013b. "The Translation of Kutiyattam into National and World Heritage on the Festival Stage: Some Identity Implications." In *South Asian Festivals on the Move*, edited by Ute Hüsken and Axel Michaels, 193–225. Wiesbaden: Harrassowitz.

Lukose, Ritty. 2009. *Liberalization's Children: Gender, Youth, and Consumer Citizenship in India.* Durham, NC: Duke University Press.

Mascia-Lees, Frances E. 2011. "Aesthetic Embodiment and Commodity Capitalism." In *A Companion to the Anthropology of the Body and Embodiment*, edited by Frances E. Mascia-Lees, 3–23. Oxford: Wiley-Blackwell.

Mazzarella, William. 2003. *Shoveling Smoke: Advertising and Globalization in Contemporary India.* Durham, NC: Duke University Press.

Merleau-Ponty, Maurice. 1964. *The Primacy of Perception*. Translated by Carleton Dallery. Evanston, IL: Northwestern University Press.

Moser, Heike. 2008. *Nannyar-Kuttu: Ein Teilaspekt des Sanskrittheaterkomplexes Kutiyattam*. Drama und Theater in Südasien 6. Wiesbaden: Harrassowitz.

———, ed. 2011. "Kutiyattam: 10 Years after the UNESCO Declaration." Special issue, *Indian Folklife* 38.

Narayanan, Mundoli. 2006. "Overritualization of Performance: Western Discourses on Kutiyattam." *TDR: The Drama Review* 50 (2): 136–53.

Osella, Filippo, and Caroline Osella. 2003. "Migration and the Commoditization of Ritual: Sacrifice, Spectacle, and Contestations in Kerala, India." *Contributions to Indian Sociology* 37 (1–2): 109–39.

———. 2006. "Once Upon a Time in the West? Stories of Migration and Modernity from Kerala, South India." *Journal of the Royal Anthropological Institute* 12:569–88.

Oza, Rupal. 2006. *The Making of Neoliberal India: Nationalism, Gender, and the Paradoxes of Globalization*. New York: Routledge.

Parayil, Govindan, ed. 2000. *Kerala: The Development Experience, Reflections on Sustainability and Replicability*. London: Zed.

Raja, K. Kunjunni. 1974. "Kootiyattam: A General Survey." *National Centre for the Performing Arts: Quarterly Journal* 3 (2): 1–14.

———. 2001. Introduction to *Bhasa Afresh: New Problems in Bhasa Plays*, by N.P. Unni, ix–xiii. Delhi: Nag.

Sangari, Kumkum, and Sudesh Vaid. 1989. "Recasting Women: An Introduction." In *Recasting Women: Essays in Colonial History*, edited by Kumkum Sangari and Sudesh Vaid, 1–26. New Delhi: Kali for Women.

Sastri, Ganapati T., ed. 1915. *The Svapnavasavadatta of Bhasa*. 2nd ed. Trivandrum: Trivandrum Government Press.

Smith, Laurajane. 2006. *Uses of Heritage*. London: Routledge.

SNA (Sangeet Natak Akademi). 1953–58; 1974–75; 1991–92. *Annual Reports*. Delhi: Sangeet Natak Akademi.

———. 1995. *Kutiyattam Mahotsavam Booklet*. New Delhi: Sangeet Natak Akademi.

Sowle, John Stevens. 1982. "The Traditions, Training, and Performance of Kutiyattam, Sanskrit Drama in South India." PhD diss., University of California, Berkeley.

Sreekumar, Sharmila. 2007. "The Land of Gender Paradox: Getting Past the Commonsense of Contemporary Kerala." *Inter-Asia Cultural Studies* 8 (1): 34–54.

Taylor, Diana. 2003. *The Archive and the Repertoire: Performing Cultural Memory in the Americas*. Durham, NC: Duke University Press.

Thomas, Sonja. 2011. "From Chattas to Churidars: Syrian Christian Religious Minorities in a Secular Indian State." PhD diss., State University of New Jersey, Rutgers.

UNESCO 2001. First Proclamation of Masterpieces of the Oral and Intangible Heritage of Humanity. Paris: UNESCO.

———. 2003. Convention for the Safeguarding of the Intangible Cultural Heritage of Humanity. Paris: UNESCO.

———. 2007. "Kutiyattam Japan-Funds-in-Trust Terminal Report." Unpublished.

Unni, N. P. 2001. *Bhasa Afresh: New Problems in Bhasa Plays*. Delhi: Nag.

Zachariah, K. C., B. A. Prakash, and Rajan S. Irudaya. 2002. "Gulf Migration Study: Employment, Wages, and Working Conditions of Kerala Migrants in the United Arab Emirates." Trivandrum Centre for Development Studies Working Paper No. 326.

LEAH LOWTHORP is College Fellow in Folklore and Mythology at Harvard University. Her work takes a postcolonial approach to cosmopolitanism, UNESCO intangible cultural heritage, and the politics of culture in India.

2 The Economic Imperative of UNESCO Recognition: A South Korean Shamanic Ritual

THIS STUDY EXAMINES a South Korean shamanic ritual to explore how UNESCO recognition complicates preexisting discourses concerning the interface of cultural and economic values in heritage making and heritage maintenance. Although UNESCO seldom discusses the economic issues associated with heritage status, financial factors are a key concern and a source of tension among local and national stakeholders when valorizing selected local culture for translocal use and recognition. Local perceptions and use of the global project are closely related to the goals and protocols of the 2003 ICH Convention.

Location: Cheju Island, South Korea

The designated ritual comes from Cheju (Jeju) Island, located in Korea's southern sea (figure 1). Both the largest island and the smallest province in Korea, Cheju is 39.8 miles wide and 45.4 miles long, with a total area of 713 square miles. Mount Halla, the highest mountain in South Korea, stands at the center of this volcanic island. As of 2014, approximately six hundred thousand people (1.2 percent of the South Korean population) live on Cheju. Due to its exquisite beauty, Cheju Island has become one of the most popular tourist destinations in the nation. In 2007, UNESCO designated several World Natural Heritage sites on the island; the organization had already named Cheju as a Biosphere Reserve in 2002, and more recently, in 2010, it was designated a Global Geopark. Thus, the phrase "UNESCO Triple Crown" is featured on the provincial government's English website.[1] Unsurprisingly, the island has been attracting an increasing number of foreigners.

Cheju was once an independent kingdom called T'amna but was subjugated by the mainland's Koryŏ dynasty in the thirteenth century.

41

Cheju

FIGURE 1
Map of Korea with Cheju Island indicated.

During the subsequent Chosŏn dynasty (1392–1910), the island was a destination for exiles and was considered by mainland elites as Korea's internal other, a place lacking civilization. For example, the exile Kim Chŏng (1486–1521) observed in his *Cheju p'ungt'orok* (Cheju topography), "Only a few are literate"; "their minds are vulgar"; "they have no sense of honor or justice" (Jeju Cultural Center 2007, 17).[2] The sixteenth-century text *Sinjŭng Tongguk yŏji sŭngnam* (Newly verified survey of the geography of the Eastern Kingdom, hereafter *Sinjŭng*) offers a comprehensive survey of Cheju, including its customs (Minjok Munhwa Ch'ujinhoe [1530] 1969, 96–97).

Several local characteristics emphasized in these reports are also well known to present-day South Koreans: the island's warm weather, the excess of women in the population, and the islanders' distinct dialect, long lives, flourishing shamanic practices, and distinctive custom of constructing walls of stacked volcanic stones. Scholar-officials from the mainland often noted the prevalence of shamanism in Cheju and pointed to it as evidence of the region's backwardness. Observing that shamanic practice in Cheju was one hundred times more popular than it was on the mainland and construing this as evidence of the region's cultural lag, the hard-nosed Neo-Confucian governor Yi Hyŏngsang (1653–1733) destroyed 129 shrines in 1702.

During the Japanese colonial period (1910–45), the word *superstition* facilitated an active and purposeful suppression of shamanic practice throughout Korea. Reform-minded nationalist organizations vehemently criticized shamanism in a nationwide campaign that reached outlying Cheju Island. During this time, for example, the youth organization of Ojo-ri in southern Cheju discussed the harm of the Spirit Worshipper's Guild and unanimously decided to prevent shamanic rituals in their village (*Tonga ilbo* 1922). At the same time, the view that shamanism is a Korean spiritual practice emerged. Some intellectuals championed an essentialized and nationalized form of the previously vilified vernacular religion.

These contradictory views of shamanism persisted in postliberation South Korea and continue to be touted by various groups. These views have been fundamental to interpretive efforts by scholars, activists, and the government, who all came to use shamanism in their own ways and for their own purposes. At the turn of the new millennium, indigeneity became a cultural commodity pressed into the service of the neoliberal economy: select shamanic rituals from the island were displayed for a "global" audience during the 2002 World Cup (Yun 2006), and local and national stakeholders made great efforts to ensure that a Cheju ritual was added to UNESCO's Representative List of the Intangible Cultural Heritage of Humanity.

ICH Element: The Yŏngdŭng Rite at the Ch'ilmŏri Shrine

These local and national efforts succeeded, as UNESCO added a shamanic ritual from Cheju to its Representative List of the Intangible Cultural Heritage of Humanity in the fall of 2009. The designated cultural element is called the Yŏngdŭng Rite because it is dedicated to Yŏngdŭng, the goddess of wind. This goddess is believed to visit the island during the first half of the second lunar month (on dates that usually fall in March). Sea workers such as diving women and fishermen generally wish for their safety and for a good catch, so it is they who hire shamans and prepare offerings for the goddess.

Indigenous Cheju shamans are called *simbang*. These generally hereditary practitioners are first and foremost perceived as ritual specialists, those who can perform *kut* (large-scale shamanic rituals) in traditional Cheju style. Simbang take pride in their competence in

ritual performance, which requires talent in singing, dancing, and
theatrical playing, in addition to reciting prodigious repertoires of
ritual speech, both learned and improvised. As for-hire specialists,
contemporary shamans receive legal tender for their services and take
home liberal offerings including cash and sacrificial foods such as rice,
fruit, and meat.[3] In recent decades nonhereditary migrant shamans
from the mainland have become dominant in Cheju's vernacular religious market. Because they are not originally from Cheju, they are
disqualified from heritage projects. However, their services are in
demand among islanders who care more about ritual efficacy than
the essentialized sense of local tradition advocated by social elites.
While some simbang construe them as a threat, others collaborate
with these migrant shamans in an effort to expand their professional
opportunities. Thus, migrant shamans give rise to the dispute over
authenticity in which the island's identity and heritage are formulated
and defined (cf. Scher 2002, 480).

The Yŏngdŭng Rite selected for the designation is performed at
the Ch'ilmŏri Shrine located on the slopes of Sara Peak in the eastern
part of Cheju City. It is marked by three spirit stones placed side by
side in an open area ringed by pines—shamanic shrines are typically
outdoors in sites without roofs or walls, but marked by spirit trees or
stones. A rather simple rite is performed on the first day of the second
lunar month to welcome the goddess, and a more grand-scale rite is
performed at the shrine a fortnight later. This latter ritual receives far
broader attention from the media as well as the local populace and
UNESCO officials.

The earliest record of the Yŏngdŭng Rite is found in *Sinjŭng*:

> On the first day of February, people in Kwidŏk, Kimnyŏg, etc., set up
> twelve wooden poles to welcome the deity [of the wind] and make
> sacrifices to her. People in Aewŏl make rafts [whose floating platform
> is] shaped like a horse's head, decorate them with colorful fabric, and
> entertain the deity by performing the Yangmahŭi.[4] This ceremony is
> called Yŏndŭng[5] and ends on the fifteenth [of February]. Sailing on
> a ship is prohibited during the month. (Minjok Munhwa Ch'ujinhoe
> [1530] 1969, 95–96)

This excerpt has been quoted by a variety of sources: in records by
those who sojourned in Cheju during the Chosŏn period, in today's
academic works about the island, and in folkloric materials and festival

pamphlets that place a high value on the longevity of contemporary practices.

The elaborate annual ritual has a complex procedure whose bare outlines I have extracted from a book published by the Association for the Ch'ilmŏri Yŏngdŭng Rite Preservation (hereafter Association 2005, 37–54).[6] Although devoted mainly to the goddess Yŏngdŭng, the ritual embraces all deities. As do all shamanic rituals, it begins with the lead simbang inviting deities, including the shrine deities, to the altar. Then the simbang entertains them. The next session is devoted to the dragon kings and the goddess Yŏngdŭng. In the following session, called "scattering seeds," divers go out into the ocean and scatter millet (representing the seeds of sea products such as seaweed and abalone), and the lead simbang offers divinations about the sea harvest. Then a simbang forestalls village misfortunes, and several simbang offer divinations for each participant's family members. The ensuing antics between the lead simbang and seven playful male deities called *Yŏnggam* lighten up the atmosphere. Following this, shamans sing a song called "Sŏujet-sori" led by the chief shaman, while all participants dance. It is believed that humans and gods can be united through dancing and singing. Then ritual sponsors set miniature straw boats adrift in the sea. Finally, the lead simbang sends back all invited deities and spirits.

Current Status with Regard to UNESCO: The Sole South Korean Shamanic Ritual to Achieve UNESCO Recognition

UNESCO added the Yŏngdŭng Rite performed at the Ch'ilmŏri Shrine to its Representative List of the Intangible Cultural Heritage of Humanity in fall 2009. As of 2015, a total of seventeen South Korean elements had been recognized by UNESCO. Among the ten regional shamanic rituals that the South Korean government designated as Important Intangible Cultural Property (*chungyo muhyŏng munhwajae*) between 1980 and 1996, this Cheju ritual is the only one that has earned UNESCO recognition. One administrator in the provincial office observed that the Yŏngdŭng Rite achieved world heritage status because its uniqueness and scholarly merit were globally recognized (Kim Hoch'ŏn 2013). This popular view assumes that the rite has an inherently superior value to other cultural practices. However,

examining the process by which it won the global certification makes
it plain that, as many scholars of heritage studies have shown (e.g.,
Noyes 2006; Smith and Akagawa 2009), world heritage is *made*.

Selection and award discussions generally marginalize the economic aspects of world heritage, "as if economic considerations might
besmirch or spoil the purity of heritage" (Bendix 2009, 258). However,
the reality indicates otherwise. UNESCO is a poorly endowed UN
agency and financially dependent on wealthy states to support cultural
causes.[7] Boosting tourism is a major motivation for national and local
stakeholders who nominate local elements for UNESCO inscription
(Bendix 2009, 258; Hafstein 2009, 106; Kirshenblatt-Gimblett 1998;
Yúdice 2003). The case of the Cheju ritual follows suit. Although the
promise of increased symbolic capital in relation to other nations is
certainly an important motivation for pursuing international recognition, financial interests are also important.

The nomination process involved a four-pronged effort by a folklorist, the shamans, the Provincial Government, and the Cultural
Heritage Administration (CHA, the state-sanctioned governing body
that oversees traditional culture in South Korea). While the provincial government and the CHA initiated and oversaw the nomination,
folklorist Mun Mubyŏng, well known for his research on Cheju shamanism, prepared the content of the dossier. The CHA sent a crew
of camera operators and cinematographers to the island to film the
ritual. These textual and visual materials, required in support of a
nomination, present the island as an isolated, ultra-rural, and timeless shamanic enclave.

Unfamiliar with a procedure involving formal protocols, the shamans of the Association were little interested at first in nominating
the rite for the foreign institution, but in the end they participated. A
few weeks before the final UNESCO decision was made in Abu Dhabi,
the members of the Association conducted a ceremony to pray for the
ritual's election. The skill holder of the Yŏngdŭng Rite and his two
trainees accepted the English-language consent form agreeing to
the ritual's nomination and conceding their rights to the materials.
Although all concerned parties had agreed on nominating the ritual
for global recognition, there was little communication among them
regarding how it would help to safeguard the "dying" tradition or who
would be best served by the outcome. While the application materials

do not hint at the economic value of UNESCO recognition, the topic was discussed openly in domestic contexts. As we shall see, this lack of communication created tension among the various parties involved in nominating the Cheju ritual.

On-the-Ground Perspectives:
What Is Gained and Who Gains?

What then was the effect of the UNESCO recognition? Although my observations are limited and it is still rather early to say how events will unfold, a few points are noteworthy. Immediately after the ritual's inscription on the Representative List, all concerned parties seemed to revel in the global recognition, as though the UNESCO fairy would magically shower benefits upon the island and Korea. Numerous contradictions that had been smothered by this initial excitement soon emerged, dimming the anticipated glory and diffusing the promised economic benefits.

As with other potential awardees, one of the local and national stakeholders' primary agendas for the nomination was "to secure a source of recognition and revenue for" the island and the country (Scher 2002, 465). Unsurprisingly, the most noticeable effort was made toward this end, resulting in intensified other-orientedness: the imperative was to exhibit and celebrate, for a broader audience, a ritual that is no longer very relevant to the majority of contemporary islanders' lives (cf. Foster 2011). No one disputed that the island's new international standing should be publicized by making it known at various venues and in a variety of contexts. The debates mostly focused on *how* this should be accomplished.

Although not entirely new, this other-orientedness was clear even at the annual daylong farewell rite performed at the Ch'ilmŏri Shrine on March 29, 2010 (figure 2). While I observed other types of public rituals during my yearlong fieldwork from fall 2001 to summer 2002, I had missed the Yŏngdŭng Rite due to other research commitments. The 2010 performance was the first time that I had observed the entire ritual since seeing part of it as an amateur onlooker in 1997. Therefore, I do not claim that all that I witnessed that day was a direct consequence of the UNESCO recognition; still, it was clear that the designation mattered. When I approached the ceremonial space

FIGURE 2
Yŏngdŭng Rite at the Ch'ilmŏri Shrine on March 29, 2010. Photograph by
author.

that morning, the ritual skill holder was facing away from me. I was
struck by the fact that his hair had turned quite gray. Although it
had been a few years since I had last seen him, I was surprised: in the
video submitted in support of the ritual's nomination in 2008, his hair
was jet black. His wife, who now referred to her husband as Master
(*sŏnsaengnim*), later explained to me, "He stopped dyeing his hair on
purpose." The shock of gray hair surely made him look more dignified
and thus more appropriate to his new status.

Although camera operators, journalists, and scholars have long
been regulars at public rituals, on this occasion their presence was
almost overwhelming. Cheju branches of KBS and MBC, two of the
most popular nationwide television stations, were filming the entire
ritual with huge cameras, and many scholars and journalists were
clicking away with their cameras and recording videos of the performance. In fact, the crowd of journalists and scholars, who far
outnumbered diving women and shipowners' wives, made up most
of the audience. But the sense of a potential audience was present.

Shamans are always necessarily attuned to the expectations of their audience, but under these circumstances the gaze of an expanded and unknown audience, whether copresent or imagined, was obviously felt. Although it was still March, the sunlight was a bit too strong to bear for those sitting without shade. As usual in public events, elderly shamans just sat in front, without contributing much to the performance. One of them had improvised a hat made of newspapers, but the lead shaman instructed her to take it off; while perfectly functional from her vantage point, it was not aesthetically suitable for images that might appear on television.

For audiences unfamiliar with the rite, the Association was selling a book about the ritual. Folklorist Mun had transcribed simbang's recitations of ritual songs and detailed the rite's history and performance procedure for the publication. The Association also distributed free booklets, with content distilled from Mun's book, that had been written in Korean, English, and Japanese. A small group of Japanese tourists showed up for a fleeting visit, and the members of the Association eagerly handed them the Japanese version of the booklet. The scholar's canonized representation and interpretation of the ritual has been parroted in newspapers, magazines, and governmental and nongovernmental heritage literature. Thus, Mun has exerted a great deal of discursive power.

Besides the Association's voluntary effort to promote the ritual, there was also outside pressure to do so. As with the World Cup (Yun 2006), despite heightened expectations the ritual did not win a broader audience from outside the island. The Japanese tourists shouted "Great!" (*sugoi*) but soon disappeared with their tour guide, headed to their next destination. The English booklets were all wasted because there were no native English-speaking members of the audience that year. Still, blind to pragmatic matters, local cultural brokers had pressured the Association to make the event more inclusive of the imagined global audience; an artist opined that the Association should produce booklets in additional languages in order to make the ritual truly global. Mr. Kim, who manages all practical matters for the shaman association, asked, "Where would the money come from [to get them all translated]—and for what?" Seeing that only three straw boats were being released at the end of the event, one scholar remarked that a global ritual warranted far more—the UNESCO status meant to him that the rite is now global. In a rather irritated tone of voice, Mr. Kim responded that it was difficult to find straw, since few locals still farmed.

To promote the ritual's new status, cultural and economic policy-making agencies also sponsored staged performances. In September 2010, for instance, several members of the Association performed a small portion of the ritual for the event "Let's Go to See Good" (*kut porŏ kaja*) at the Cheju Art Center.[8] As the intriguing title suggests, this was a heritage campaign event intended to show the public that traditional performances such as Buddhist dances (*sŭngmu*) and epic songs (*p'ansori*) are "good" to see, just as kut were in the past when few other entertainment opportunities were available. Altogether, eight groups from the mainland and the island, five of which had been recognized as national intangible cultural treasures, performed in a ninety-minute event.[9]

Although I missed the event itself, I did hear a few reactions to it. Mun did not conceal his chagrin that he had not been invited to an affair featuring the ritual he had transformed into a world cultural asset. Kim voiced displeasure at the high-handed institution's poor management of the event. The staff kept requesting that the ritual be shortened to fit the time frame for the whole event, a demand hardly new for staged performances. In the end, simbang were pushed to perform for twenty minutes total, a situation Kim compared with abbreviating Shakespeare's play *Romeo and Juliet* to four words: "Oh, Romeo! Oh, Juliet!" From his view, it was nearly impossible to show anything meaningful from the daylong ritual in such a short time and thus compromised the shamans' mission of displaying the authentic tradition anticipated by the audience. In such a show, he said straight-forwardly, simbang are "used as commodities." He also hinted at ego battles among the stellar performers: the staff members designated a smaller, shabby dressing room for sixteen simbang while assigning better and more spacious rooms to groups from the mainland. The staff used the excuse that local performers should yield the better dressing rooms to those from the mainland because they could be viewed as guests, but to Kim, this move subordinated the shamans to the other performers.

The Association was also mobilized to perform in the National Center for Korean Traditional Performing Arts (NCKTPA) in Seoul. The ritual was on the list of the center's "2010 Saturday Premium Performances" (*t'oyo myŏngp'um kongyŏn*) series featuring traditional performing arts. Embedded in the title is a vision of cultural practices as high-quality objects—the Korean word *myŏngp'um* refers to "a fine article, gem, or a masterpiece." The host of the series, the National Kugak (traditional Korean music) Center, scheduled the fourth Saturday of each month exclusively for performing art genres recognized by UNESCO, including the Yŏngdŭng Rite for October, and made an effort to lure diverse audiences to the "heritage goods" (Bendix 2009, 255–58). If not actually free, the admission fee was very reasonable: the general admission was ten thousand wŏn (about nine US dollars) with various discount options. One such option catering to foreign visitors offered a twenty percent discount for Korean Air passengers visiting Korea. One of the online media blurbs highlighted the advantage of observing the island's ritual without actually going there: "Experience the Cheju Ch'ilmŏri Yŏngdŭng Rite in Seoul."[10] Regional and national decision-making bodies thus used the Cheju kut as "a good of morally and economically enhanced valence" (Bendix 2009, 264), a promotional practice not incongruent with the UNESCO ideal of opening up distinctly local practices for the world.

These multitudinous efforts by state-sponsored cultural organizations to promote the island's kut reveal the events' marginality for the general public. In fact, about half of the seats of the rather small hall were empty for the performance in Seoul. Thus, anticipated symbolic and practical benefits—status and revenue—were not realized (cf. Noyes 2003). Although one of the male performers said that the ritual is an event in which the audience and the performers interact, most onlookers seemed estranged. They were trying to grasp what was happening on the stage by reading digital subtitles on the monitor hung high on the front wall. As nobody from the audience would come up to the stage for an exorcism, the female simbang beckoned to one of her own young performers, a recourse I had never seen in public performances. In an effort to help, I went onto the stage as a living prop. At the segment when the audience was supposed to dance with the simbang on the stage, most members of the audience remained in their seats. Some young female students were amused by one male student moving his arms and shoulders like the performers. This awkward scene was in stark contrast to the enthusiasm aroused by the music and dance routines of K-pop singers.

Nonetheless, stakeholders cannot simply let their hard-earned opportunity be squandered: if consumers lack interest in the ritual, perhaps it can be cultivated through education. In February 2013, the province announced its plan to build two new halls to be used for training, exhibitions, and performances. The provincial administration went so far as to lift development constraints to allow the new construction. Whereas the shrine moved to its current location in order to make way for the construction of other structures in the past (Chang 1983, 108), the heritage regime is now prepared to alter the cultural and physical landscape to highlight the ritual that takes place there. The news of new buildings was replete with a preservation discourse. The buildings are called *chŏnsu hoegwan*, or halls for passing heritage. Conceptualized almost as a museum to preserve objects, the buildings were construed as safeguarding the rite's future. The provincial office announced that the purpose of the halls was to promote the excellence of Cheju's shamanic myths and intangible culture (Hwang 2013). However, these proclamations raise the question of exactly how and for whom the buildings will help safeguard the ritual.

Discussion: An Uncertain Glory

Many cultural pundits and commentators focus on the transmission of objectified ritual lore and skills from old to young simbang, but there is little discussion about how to continue the annual ceremony when the motivation for its very existence has faded. Development on the island has taken away many of the jobs of the diving ladies, the ritual's "real owners" as identified in the nomination dossier.[11] Moreover, they are not interested in passing their difficult and dangerous job on to their daughters. On a practical level, most villages no longer have a need to sponsor the ritual, and only a few are now in any way concerned with its practice. In 1981 diving ladies and fishermen's wives from some 150 households participated in the Yŏngdŭng Rite at the Ch'ilmŏri Shrine (Kim Sunam 1983, 18), but in the 2010 ritual only a dozen sponsors were present. Because of the decreased number of the faithful, in combination with the ritual's symbolic position on the island and in the nation, the provincial office became the main sponsors. In 2010, according to Mr. Kim, it supplied 2 million wŏn (about 1,800 US dollars) to the Association, which in turn provided the diving ladies with 100,000 wŏn (about 90 US dollars) to aid with the food offerings. Lack of active participation by the former clients presents a serious challenge to the Association's efforts to maintain the annual rite as something more than a mere display. How the organization might do this remains unclear. As is true of most safe-guarded heritage practices, the immediate mission is to keep the performances going regardless of whether they actually relate to anyone's internal beliefs.

The prevalent preservation discourse also ignores the very nature of shamans' training. Simbang have learned their multifaceted skills by observing the performances of more experienced simbang and their clients' behavior, as well as by performing their assigned roles in a motley array of ritual situations. The general decrease in demand for simbang's rituals, both communal and individual, deprives apprentice simbang of these opportunities. While context-sensitive interactional skills with clients and with the supernatural cannot be learned in training halls, the new buildings will be helpful for teaching a younger generation other routine performance skills such as singing and danc-ing. The Association will have separate space for exhibiting material objects and photos and for performing the ritual for broad audiences. This direction is part and parcel of the heritage tourism promoted by the local and the national governments and tacitly supported by UNESCO. Perhaps these preservation halls might someday even find their way onto tourist maps.

When the ritual was first inscribed on the Representative List in 2009, Kim Yunsu, the skill holder of the Ch'ilmŏri Yŏngdŭng Rite, seemed to bask in the glory of media attention. While conferring with politicians and local elites who were celebrating the ritual's elevated status and planning how to utilize the invested economic good, he recounted the social ostracism that he had experienced as a young simbang and expressed his hope that the global recognition would change people's attitude toward simbang (Chin 2009). So have sim-bang, as Kim Yunsu wished, acquired new dignity with UNESCO's validation of the ritual?

Not necessarily. In March 2011, a local assemblyman from the rul-ing Grant National Party decried as "superstition" the shamanic ritual to be performed at the memorial service for the April Third Event.[12] Still, the UNESCO designation does offer some aid when responding to public denunciations. The assemblyman's comments sparked an outcry from several local organizations, including the Association (Yi 2011). These organizations issued a lengthy statement inveigh-ing against his affront to the victims' memory, using the UNESCO sanction to support their argument that the politician's dismissal of a kut that has become the heritage of the world's people (*illyu yusan*) was out of touch. The fact that the advocates of the practitioner and the popular religion borrowed the authority of the supranational institution underscores the operation of hierarchy of value. The titles undoubtedly helped to raise simbang's social position, but they do not completely erase their stigma. The insensitive remark made by the politician bespeaks the tenacity of public prejudice toward shamans. The simbang's situation is quite different from others involved in intangible cultural heritage who are eager to learn, for example, traditional music and dance with the aspiration of becoming respected artists (*yesurin*) after receiving university-based training. Referring to a non-simbang member of the Association pursuing a PhD in Korean Studies at Cheju National University, a local intellectual said to me, "Who would want to become a simbang?"

The CHA planned the ritual's UNESCO inscription on the list not so much to improve simbang's social position but rather to reap its symbolic and economic value. In 2013, the ritual was selected for the CHA's nationwide project "Living Cultural Assets Project" (*saeng saeng munhwajae saŏp*), implemented in 2008 with the goal of revitalizing the local economy through heritage tourism.[13] In March 2013, the CHA announced that the project resulted in an economic jolt to the service sectors, such as transportation, lodging, and food, of as much as 3.3 times the original investment (CHA 2013b). Although how they reached this conclusion is unknown, the central and provincial governments certainly were in need of providing recognizable evidence of success in heritage promotion. It is not clear whether the Yŏngdŭng Rite will also bring about rosy economic results. My observations of the ritual at the Ch'ilmŏri Shrine and at the NCKTPA suggest a mismatch between sellers and buyers of the cultural product. In the age of consumer electronics, many other forms of entertainment are distracting Koreans from the charm that shamanic rituals once held. While shamans' magical intervention continues to be sought in private by a wide range of Koreans who live in an exceedingly uncertain contemporary society (e.g., Kendall 2009; Kim Seong-nae 2002), these clients seem to be far less interested in the wonders of staged shamanic rituals.

In the extreme, the ritual's global recognition strips the shamans and their clients of the option to cease the ritual, which many seashore villages on Cheju have already done. Although the incumbent skill holder has reached the pinnacle of his profession, the Association's office manager pointed out, future generations of the Association will feel it even more burdensome to maintain the public event. The honor also brought some financial disadvantages to the lead shaman, whose wife complained, "People don't hire him anymore because they assume he will be too expensive now that he is a world-famous shaman. This is so unfair that I should write a letter to UNESCO." She indicated both that their assumption about his higher fees is false and that UNESCO cost him a significant portion of his livelihood. Ironically, while shamans' use of their practice to enhance their own economic and symbolic interest remains suspect in the public imagination, making the island ritual world heritage and utilizing it as resource is justified in the name of local and national identities and economic benefits. Thus, the Cheju case calls for reflection about the moral, intellectual, and practical implications of UNESCO intervention.

Acknowledgments

This essay is a product of my long engagement with the people of Cheju Island who generously shared their time and insights into local shamanism. Their perspectives gave a voice to and shaped the essay. The coeditors of the volume, Michael Dylan Foster and Lisa Gilman, and the anonymous reviewers offered helpful suggestions to improve an earlier version of the essay. My long-time mentor Roger L. Janelli posed perceptive questions, and Danille Elise Christensen made my writing flow more smoothly. The Kyujanggak Fellowship of Seoul National University and the Residential Scholar Program of Korea University International Center for Korean Studies allowed me to conduct research in Korea during the 2009–11 academic years. The University of Kansas General Research Fund provided me with funding to concentrate on completing the paper in the summer of 2013. An earlier version of this essay was presented at annual meetings of the American Folklore Society and the American Anthropological Association and at a Tea and Talk organized by the Center for East Asian Studies at the University of Kansas. I am grateful to all of these individuals and institutions.

Notes

1. The "About Jeju" portion of the island's official promotional website (http://english.jeju.go.kr/) features a page called "UNESCO Triple Crown of Jeju" as part of its "Beautiful Jeju" section. The site praises Cheju as the "only place on Earth to receive all three UNESCO designations in natural sciences."

2. All transliterations and English translations are mine.

3. Although established simbang have a certain number of fixed rituals conducted annually, additional ritual opportunities are contingent upon clients' needs.

4. *Yangmahŭi* literally means "the play of jumping horses." Hyŏn Yongjun (1980) surmised that it referred to the playful raft race conducted as part of the Yŏngdŭng Rite. At the end of the ritual, each man took his raft carrying a miniature rice-straw boat laden with sacrificial objects out to sea and set it on the waves to float away as the deity made her departure from the island. The one who steered his raft fastest and released the miniature boat first was the winner, and it was believed that he would have the largest catch of fish during the year.

5. The standard pronunciation of the Chinese characters 燃燈 in the original text would be *yŏndŭng*, but this is both written and pronounced *yŏngdŭng* in shamanic contexts in Cheju today.

6. Most members of the Association are simbang.

7. I am grateful to the anonymous reviewer for directing my attention to this point. For backstage politics regarding this issue, see Valdimar Tr. Hafstein's 2009 study.

8. Note the punning in the Korean phrase 굿 보러 가자, which has been used for some time to advertise various traditional performance genres. Here, 굿 is the Korean transliteration of the English word *good* rather than *shamanic rituals*, for which the English transliteration is *kut*.

9. This free event was organized by Cheju City and the Korean Cultural Heritage Foundation under the sponsorship of the CHA.

10. "Sŏul esŏ Cheju Ch'ilmŏri-dang Yŏngdŭng-kut ŭl kyŏnghŏm hae poseyo." Accessible at http://www.newswire.co.kr/newsRead.php?no=496643.

11. The number of diving women in Cheju has been rapidly decreasing—14,143 were active in this profession in 1970 (An Mi-Jeong 2008, 72), but only 4,995 in 2010 (about one-third of the 1970 number); in 2010 only two divers were young women in their thirties, and 70 percent were in their sixties and seventies. This drastic decrease of divers, who have been praised as representing the strong spirit of Cheju women, generated an urgent desire to safeguard their culture. In 2006, a museum dedicated to diving women opened in Hado-ri in northeast Cheju, and the stakeholders of the island are aiming to have their culture added to the UNESCO list (Kang 2011).

12. The violent conflicts between leftist insurgents and rightist counterinsurgents were triggered by the left-led uprising on April 3, 1948, and led to massive civilian deaths: at least thirty thousand people, or one-tenth of the island's population at that time, were killed (Cumings 2005, 219–21).

13. The ritual was one of forty-five selected items out of a total of ninety-six applications submitted by municipal governments in South Korea (CHA 2013a).

References Cited

An Mi-Jeong. 2008. *Cheju Chamsu ŭi padabat: Sahoe kwan'gye wa saengt'aejŏk chisok kanŭngsŏng ŭl wihan munhwajŏk silch'ŏn* [The maritime garden of Jeju woman divers: Social relations and cultural creativity for the sustainable environment]. Cheju: Jeju National University Press.

Association for the Ch'ilmŏri Shrine Yŏngdŭng Rite Preservation. 2005. *Param ŭi ch'ukche, Ch'ilmŏri-dang Yŏngdŭng-kut* [The festival of wind, the Yŏngdŭng Rite at the Ch'ilmŏri Shrine], with Mun Mubyŏng's transcriptions and explanations of the [oral] materials. Seoul: Gold Egg.

Bendix, Regina. 2009. "Heritage between Economy and Politics: An Assessment from the Perspective of Cultural Anthropology." In *Intangible Heritage*, edited by Laurajane Smith and Natsuko Akagawa, 253–69. New York: Routledge.

CHA (Cultural Heritage Administration of Korea). 2013a. "Munhwajaech'ŏng 2013 nyŏn saeng saeng munhwajae saŏp sŏnjŏng palp'yo" [CHA selects and announces the 2013 living cultural assets]. http://www.cha.go.kr/newsBbz /selectNewsBbzView.do?newsItemId=155698068&sectionId=b_sec_1&pageIndex =112&pageUnit=10&strWhere=&strValue=&sdate=&edate=&category=&mn =NS_01_02.

———. 2013b. "Munhwajaech'ŏng saeng saeng munhwajae saŏp, 3.3 pae ŭi kyŏgjaejŏk p'agŭp hyogwa ch'angch'ul" [CHA's living cultural assets project resulted in an economic jolt of as much as 3.3 times the original investment]. http://www.cha.go.kr/newsBbz/selectNewsBbzView.do?newsItemId=155698125 &sectionId=b_sec_1&pageIndex=107&pageUnit=10&strWhere=&strValue=& sdate=&edate=&category=&mn=NS_01_02.

Chang Chugŭn. 1983. "Kanginhan sam ŭi hyŏnjang, p'ungyo ŭi kiwŏn" [The resilient life, wishes for abundant harvest]. In *Han'guk ŭi Kut 3, Cheju-do Yŏngdŭng Kut*, edited by Chang Chugŭn and Yi Pohyŏng, 95–116. Seoul: Yŏlhwadang.

Chin Sŏnhŭi. 2009. "Cheju-kut insik pakkwiŏtssŭmyŏn" [Wishing a change in people's attitude toward Cheju shamanic rituals]. *Halla ilbo*, October 1, 12.

Cumings, Bruce. 2005. *Korea's Place in the Sun: A Modern History*. New York: W. W. Norton.

Foster, Michael Dylan. 2011. "The UNESCO Effect: Confidence, Defamiliarization, and a New Element in the Discourse on a Japanese Island." *Journal of Folklore Research* 48 (1): 63–107.

Hafstein, Valdimar Tr. 2009. "Intangible Heritage as a List: From the Masterpieces to Representation." In *Intangible Heritage*, edited by Laurajane Smith and Natsuko Akagawa, 93–111. New York: Routledge.

Hwang Kyŏng-gŭn. 2013. "'Cheju Ch'ilmŏri-dang Yŏngdŭng-kut' chŏnsu hoegwan kŏlliphae pojon" ['Cheju Ch'ilmŏri Shrine Yŏngdŭng Rite' will be safeguarded by building a preservation hall]. *Seoul sinmun*, May 8, 27.

Hyŏn Yongjun. 1980. "Yangmahŭi ko" [An examination of Yangmahŭi]. In *Yŏnam Hyŏn P'yŏnghyo paksa hoegap kinyŏm nonch'ong*, 679–98. Seoul: Hyŏngsŏl Ch'ulp'ansa.

Jeju Cultural Center, ed. and trans. 2007. *Cheju kogi munjip* [A collection of old records of Cheju]. Cheju: Cheju Munhwawŏn.

Kang Hong-gyun. 2011. "Haenyŏ UNESCO muhyŏng munhwa yusan tŭngjae saŏp ch'ujin" [Planning to have the diving women's culture inscribed on the list of UNESCO intangible cultural heritage of humanity]. *The Kyunghyang Shinmun*, March 7. http://news.khan.co.kr/kh_news/khan_art_view.html ?artid=201103071620331.

Kendall, Laurel. 2009. *Shamans, Nostalgias, and the IMF: South Korean Popular Religion in Motion.* Honolulu: University of Hawai'i Press.

Kim Hoch'ŏn. 2013. "Illyu yusan Cheju Ch'ilmŏri-dang Yŏngdŭng-kut chŏnsu hoegwan kŏllip twoenda" [The preservation hall will be built for the world heritage Yŏngdŭng Rite at the Ch'ilmori Shrine]. *Yŏnhap News,* February 21. http://www.yonhapnews.co.kr/culture/2013/02/21/0906000000AKR20130 221093000056.HTML.

Kim Seong-nae. 2002. "Kibok sinang ŭi yulri wa chabonjuŭi munhwa" [The ethics of shamanic fortune belief in the Korean capitalist culture]. *Chonggyo yŏn'gu* 27:61–86.

Kim Sunam. 1983. *"Ch'ilmŏri-dang Yŏngdŭng Kut"* [The Yŏngdŭng rite at the Ch'ilmŏri shrine]. In *Han'guk ŭi Kut 3, Cheju-do Yŏngdŭng Kut,* edited by Chang Chugŭn and Yi Pohyŏng, 15–54. Seoul: Yŏlhwadang.

Kirshenblatt-Gimblett, Barbara. 1998. *Destination Culture: Tourism, Museums, and Heritage.* Berkeley: University of California Press.

Minjok Munhwa Ch'ujinhoe, trans. (1530) 1969. *Sinjŭng Tongguk yŏji sŭngnam* [Newly verified survey of the geography of the eastern kingdom]. Vol. 5, no. 38. Seoul: Minjokmunhwa ch'ujinhoe.

Noyes, Dorothy. 2003. *Fire in the Plaça: Catalan Festival Politics after Franco.* Philadelphia: University of Pennsylvania Press.

———. 2006. "The Judgment of Solomon: Global Protections for Tradition and the Problem of Community Ownership." *Cultural Analysis* 5:27–56.

Scher, Philip W. 2002. "Copyright Heritage: Preservation, Carnival and the State in Trinidad." *Anthropological Quarterly* 75 (3): 453–84.

Smith, Laurajane, and Natsuko Akagawa, eds. 2009. *Intangible Heritage.* New York: Routledge.

Tonga ilbo. 1922. "Ojo ch'ŏngnyŏn ŭi il saŏp" [A project of the Ojo youth]. September 26, 4.

Yi Sŭngnok. 2011. "UNESCO illyu yusan 'Cheju ŭi kut' i misin iran marinya" [Who calls the UNESCO Intangible Cultural Heritage of Humanity a superstition?]. *Cheju ŭi sori,* March 15. http://www.jejusori.net/news/articleView .html?idxno=96945.

Yúdice, George. 2003. *The Expediency of Culture: Uses of Culture in the Global Era.* Durham, NC: Duke University Press.

Yun, Kyoim. 2006. "The 2002 World Cup and a Local Festival in Cheju: Global Dreams and the Commodification of Shamanism." *Journal of Korean Studies* 11:7–40.

KYOIM YUN is Associate Professor in the Department of East Asian Languages and Cultures at the University of Kansas.

3 Demonic or Cultural Treasure? Local Perspectives on Vimbuza, Intangible Cultural Heritage, and UNESCO in Malawi

VIMBUZA, ONE OF two Malawian dance forms inscribed on the UNESCO Representative List of the Intangible Cultural Heritage of Humanity in 2008, is a healing ritual practiced by Tumbuka people in Malawi's northern region. Vimbuza refers both to the ailments caused by Vimbuza spirits and the rituals used to heal people with these spirit-induced illnesses. Vimbuza healers diagnose and treat spirit-related illnesses in rituals that combine dress, drumming, singing, and movement. It is sometimes called a "traditional dance" and performed for entertainment rather than healing. Drawing from interviews with practitioners, the general public, and cultural sector professionals, this essay explores the implications of UNESCO recognition for Tumbuka people. Though the impact of Vimbuza's inscription on those most associated with the practice is debatable, it still has local, regional, national, and international value.

Location: Rumphi and Surrounding Districts, Northern Region, Malawi

The geographical center of the Tumbuka people and of Vimbuza is in the Rumphi District in the northern region of Malawi, a small country in south-central Africa (figure 1). Many Tumbuka people also live in the Mzimba District to the south of Rumphi. The Mashawe ritual of the neighboring Tonga ethnic group in the Nkhata Bay District is similar—many say identical—to Vimbuza (Chilivumbo 1972). Though the listing for Vimbuza on the UNESCO website does not include Mashawe, some of the documentation provided by the local UNESCO commission specifies that the two should be considered together. Other ethnic groups living in the region where Vimbuza is practiced also participate in the ritual, especially the Ngoni, who, as a result of

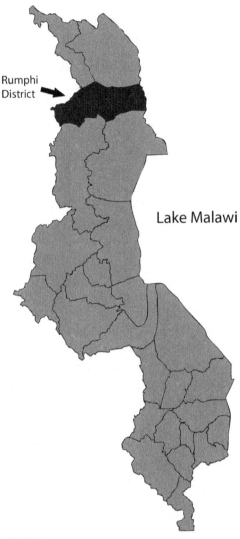

FIGURE 1
Vimbuza is practiced by the Tumbuka people who are concentrated in the Rumphi District of Malawi. Image by John Fenn.

conquest, intermarriage, and proximity, share many cultural practices with the Tumbuka. Vimbuza is also practiced in districts bordering those listed above because the district boundaries do not correlate exactly with cultural boundaries, and there are many areas where people of many cultural backgrounds live together and in close proximity.

A majority of the population of Malawi lives in rural settlements. People living in rural villages participate in a variety of occupations and have different lifestyles, though popular discourse in Malawi and across the continent positions rural life as "traditional" or "African" in juxtaposition to "modern" or "Western" ways of living associated with cities and towns. Within and on the outskirts of towns and cities are villages or village-like settlements where most people live a village lifestyle but also have easy access to town amenities and transportation. Vimbuza is mostly practiced in villages and village settlements outside towns and cities. People living in cities and towns with Vimbuza-induced ailments travel to more rural settings to be healed by Vimbuza healers.

Some tourist attractions exist in areas where Vimbuza is practiced, such as Nyika National Park near the town of Rumphi, or the city of Mzuzu, which is a crossroads for tourists traveling from the capital city Lilongwe to other tourist locations in the north or onward to Tanzania. Mzuzu boasts a small government-run museum, which featured an exhibit on Vimbuza at the time of writing that was partly funded by UNESCO. The nearby town of Nkhata Bay District along Lake Malawi attracts tourists, especially "backpackers": young, mostly European, budget travelers. Small lodges in Nkhata Bay occasionally organize performances of Mashawe. Cultural tourism is underdeveloped in Malawi, and the UNESCO Convention is motivating national efforts to develop tourism across the country that target local culture and heritage.

ICH Element: Vimbuza, A Controversial Illness and a Healing Ritual

Vimbuza refers to the illness caused by spirits that possess a person, causing a variety of physical and mental ailments, and it also refers to the rituals that are used to diagnose and heal these spirit-related illnesses.[1] Symptoms caused by spirits cannot be healed by Western medicine but rather must be treated by ritual healers. The healers gain the power to diagnose and heal spirit-related illnesses because they too are infected or possessed by the spirits; it is through their own embodied interaction with the spirits that they are able to diagnose, cure, or mitigate the symptoms of others suffering from spirit-related ailments.

The Vimbuza ritual consists of a gathering that includes one or more healers, the afflicted, family members of the afflicted, and members of the community where the ritual takes place. The ritual usually occurs outside or near the home of the healer and sometimes at a Vimbuza temple. There are several types of Vimbuza healers who have different powers and practice their healing art differently. Specific healing rituals differ; the following provides an overview of common features of rituals, all of which involve special clothing items, props, drumming, movement, and singing.

Drummers usually stand to one side of an open space. Others involved as patients, healers, and audience members stand around the periphery. The spirits dictate what happens in any given ritual,

FIGURE 2
Vimbuza performance. Enugweni, Malawi. April 2013. Photograph by author.

determining the dress, props, and other details of the event. The
healer(s) and afflicted wear special clothing, often a single-colored
red or green cotton dress for both men and women and sometimes a
hat of the same fabric decorated with large white crosses. They wear
combinations of beads around their necks, rattles around ankles,
and rattles, skins, or rags tied around their waists (figure 2). As the
drummers beat, the focal person of the event at that moment—either
a healer or a person being healed—enters into the open space. The
drumming activates the spirits in the person, who starts to move rhythmically, creating more noise with the rattles and other idiophones
on the body; the increasing noise produces an even livelier presence
of the spirits, which impels the person to move with more and more
energy. The act of moving rhythmically activates the spirits in the afflicted persons, both the healer(s) and the people seeking treatment.
As the spirits rise, the healer enters a heightened state that grants
supernatural perception beyond the typical capacity of living beings.
In this state, healers communicate with the spirits to determine the
cause of the afflicted person's ailments and to identify what the spirits
require in order to be appeased. Vimbuza rituals last for many hours
usually throughout the night.

Though Vimbuza is considered to be both a disease and a healing ritual, Vimbuza is sometimes presented in nonritual settings as a "dance" for entertainment or cultural display because it shares elements with cultural practices categorized locally as dances, or *zovina* in Chitumbuka. Some tourist venues, especially lodges and hotels that target a foreign clientele, occasionally organize nonritual Vimbuza performances for their guests. District, regional, and national cultural events that showcase dance forms from different ethnic groups sometimes feature Vimbuza in their programs. Vimbuza is also sometimes performed at political rallies alongside other dance forms to entertain politicians and the audience and to promote a political party and its leaders (Gilman 2009). These entertainment displays are different from the rituals in that the performers are not possessed, and the various elements that in the ritual are intended to interact with the spirits—drumming, rattles, and singing—are done for display. The spirits are not present; the practitioners are going through the motions to demonstrate and please rather than to achieve a ritual function.

Vimbuza is a controversial practice locally because of tensions between Western and indigenous theories of healing and between Christianity, the dominant religion in the northern region, and indigenous ancestor-based religions. Some criticize traditional healers for claiming that they can cure sick people through dance rather than sending them to the hospital where they could be cured by Western medicine. Supporters argue that the illnesses caused by spirits differ from those that can be healed through Western medicine and can only be cured through ritual. Some healers I interviewed explained that tensions with hospitals do not exist because doctors trained in Western medicine understand their limitations when it comes to spirit-related illnesses. Healer Mercy Chirwa explained that traditional and Western medicine complement one another rather than being in conflict. Healer Martha Luhanga explained that doctors at the Rumphi hospital sometimes call Winles Gondwe, the head healer of her Vimbuza temple, to tend to a patient when the doctors' treatment has failed. Gondwe then determines if the symptoms are spirit-based; if they are, the hospital releases the patient to her to be healed through ritual.

Tensions between Vimbuza and Christian churches seem to be greater than tensions with Western-style hospitals. Christian churches have long tried to suppress Vimbuza because they equate belief in spirits and rituals centered on human-spirit interaction with animism, which they consider to be antithetical to the monotheism of Christianity. Several healers I interviewed are members of the Church of Central Africa, Presbyterian (CCAP), one of the oldest and most dominant churches in the country. They explained that the CCAP bans its members from practicing Vimbuza for the reasons mentioned above. On the other hand, practitioners and those supportive of Vimbuza, many of whom are practicing Christians, believe that Vimbuza is not antithetical to Christianity. Rather, they explain that God is present at their rituals, and it is God that enables them to interact with the spirits to diagnose and heal. Within the ritual, Christian symbols and references abound: rituals begin with a Christian prayer, dresses display bold crosses, and the song lyrics are replete with Christian references. Even many of those who publicly criticize the practice because of their own Christian beliefs nevertheless secretly visit healers or "African Doctors" when hospital doctors fail to cure their illness or the sickness of a loved one (de Kok 2005).

Related to both the medical and religious controversies surrounding Vimbuza is tension over witchcraft. The Witchcraft Act, which was passed in 1911 during the colonial period, denies the existence of witchcraft and forbids cultural practices in any way associated with it (Byrne 2011; Soko and Kubik 2008). Many Malawians believe that much human suffering is the result of witchcraft, and Vimbuza healers are among those traditional healers who diagnose witchcraft and identify witches or perpetrators of witchcraft through their healing arts. The controversy over whether or not witchcraft exists and the illegality of practices aimed at identifying perpetrators further pulls Vimbuza into a controversial quagmire.

Current Status with Regard to UNESCO: One of the First Two Elements from Malawi

Vimbuza was initially proclaimed one of the ninety Masterpieces of the Oral and Intangible Heritage of Humanity by UNESCO in 2005. In 2008, UNESCO incorporated Vimbuza onto the Representative List of the Intangible Cultural Heritage of Humanity in accordance with the 2003 Convention for the Safeguarding of Intangible Cultural Heritage.[2]

The Senior Programme Officer in charge of cultural initiatives for the Malawi National Commission for UNESCO, Department of Culture staff (at the time in the Ministry of Education, Sports, and Culture), academics, and practitioners of Vimbuza contributed to the nomination process.[3] The candidature file for Vimbuza included the following items as required for the application process:

a. Map of areas where Vimbuza is practiced in Malawi

b. List of Photographs and negatives of Vimbuza Dancers

c. Letters of consent to have Vimbuza proclaimed as a masterpiece of the intangible heritage of humanity

d. Bibliography

e. 10 minute video

f. 1hr 30 minute video

g. List of practitioners[4]

Malawi comprises numerous ethnic groups and hundreds of dance practices. According to UNESCO and government officials whom I interviewed, the reason Vimbuza and Gule Wamkulu were selected for this first round largely had to do with accessibility of information that was required. Given the extensiveness of what was required for the application, selecting two cultural forms for which there was already a great deal of information was a practical decision. These two cultural forms are very vibrant and have been relatively well documented and analyzed by scholars, which facilitated compiling the extensive description, rationale, and audiovisual documentation required for the candidature file.

In the written portion of the application, Vimbuza is presented as being important to Tumbuka cultural identity, central to "the Tumbuka theory of illness," and important therapeutically, medicinally, and culturally. Given that programming instigated as a result of Vimbuza's UNESCO inscription has sometimes overemphasized Vimbuza as a form of entertainment, it is noteworthy that although the application mentions that Vimbuza both heals and entertains, it rarely references its performance outside of ritual settings. Both the initial application as well as the promotional materials that have been produced as a result of Vimbuza's inclusion on the Representative List articulate the importance of promoting Vimbuza because the controversy surrounding the practice on religious and medical grounds puts Vimbuza at risk and in greater need of cultural recognition and safeguarding. To fulfill the UNESCO mandate after its inscription, the government, in collaboration with the local UNESCO office, created a safeguarding plan that emphasized both its therapeutic and cultural value. As stipulated on the UNESCO website for Vimbuza "the safeguarding project seeks to encourage the transmission of skills and knowledge to younger generations, and raise awareness about the importance of safeguarding the Vimbuza as part of traditional health practices."[5]

Malawi is a poor country, and the government has historically provided limited resources for cultural initiatives. Malawi therefore relies heavily on donor aid to fund cultural programs. In order to pursue initiatives on its safeguarding plan, the Malawian government secured some funding from UNESCO and the Government of Japan. The planned initiatives, many of which were carried out between May 2007 and November 2009, include:

- Review of the Arts and Crafts, Museum and Monuments, and Relics acts with the aim of adding the safeguarding of ICH in the acts.
- Training of Vimbuza practitioners and chiefs on intellectual property rights, health issues associated with HIV/AIDS prevention, relationships between traditional healers and "modern medical practitioners," gender issues, and the value of formal education.
- The formation of a Vimbuza Healers and Dancers Association of Malawi was initiated "and a code of conduct established for the members as part of the counteraction against the negative image of Vimbuza caused by inappropriate practice."
- Prof. Boston Soko of Mzuzu University was charged with writing a book about Vimbuza.
- An inventory of Vimbuza practitioners was carried in the northern region.
- Two Vimbuza dance festivals were organized, one in Rumphi and one in Mzuzu, both cities in the northern region.
- A museum exhibit about Vimbuza in the Mzuzu Museum.[6]

At the time of research in 2013, the museum exhibit was still up, Professor Soko was working on the book, and no additional festivals or Vimbuza-focused events were being planned. The Vimbuza Healers and Dancers Association of Malawi was in the process of being formally constituted.

On-the-Ground Perspectives:
Satanic Practice or Valued Culture?

My presentation and discussion of "on-the-ground" perspectives is informed by the extensive literature on the 2003 ICH Convention and draws most explicitly from my interviews and less formal conversations with a variety of people with a range of educational backgrounds (from no formal schooling to university degrees) living in rural and urban settings in the region where Vimbuza is practiced. Most of these conversations occurred from February through July 2013. Among the people I interviewed in 2013 were five Vimbuza healers. I also attended several Vimbuza events to better familiarize myself with the practice. My current thinking is also informed by preliminary research I did on this topic in 2010 and my ongoing research on dance and politics in Malawi since 1995.

Based on this fieldwork, I determined that most people in the region were not familiar with UNESCO, nor did most know about UNESCO ICH initiatives or that Vimbuza had been inscribed on the UNESCO list. Two Vimbuza healers I interviewed did not know what UNESCO was but had been informed that Vimbuza had received some type of international recognition. The only healer with any substantial knowledge of UNESCO was Jejeka Chisusu Mbale, who was involved in the application process in addition to the safeguarding activities that followed.[7] After learning that Vimbuza was one of two cultural forms—and the only one from the northern region—inscribed on a UNESCO list, most interviewees expressed surprise that Vimbuza was selected over other cultural practices for a variety of reasons, the most common being that Vimbuza is a disease and a healing ritual, not a domain of "culture." This distinction raises issues about what is meant by "culture" in different contexts.

Because most were not aware of the UNESCO lists nor were they knowledgeable about the selection process, several turned the question back to me and inquired why Vimbuza had been selected. Some asked if the process had been politically motivated. Some thought the reason could have been because Vimbuza is so widely practiced in the northern region across ethnic groups, making it more representative of the northern region than some other cultural practices that are largely restricted to one ethnic group. This conclusion came after some reflection and suggested that if these individuals were to choose something to represent the northern region, they would have selected something else.

Nyakwinika, a Ngoni woman living in a village-like settlement near the city of Mzuzu, expressed that many dances exist in the north, such as the Ngoni Ingoma, that were "pure culture" and therefore would have been more appropriate. According to her, the dances that she characterized as "pure culture" express cultural identity and entertain rather than serve religious or ritual functions. She did not consider Vimbuza to be "pure culture" because it is a disease and a healing ritual—not what she considered to be a "dance" form. Traditional Authority Harry Mankhambira, at the time a head chief of the Tonga people in the Nkhata Bay District, similarly noted that the Tonga practice of Mashawe is an illness and a healing practice. Mankhambira acknowledged that although Vimbuza is part of "culture," it should not be celebrated as a form of cultural entertainment. A more appropriate option would have been something like the dance Malipenga, which is intended for entertainment and is practiced by everyone, as opposed to only those who are sick or healers. Both Nyakwinika and Mankhambira would agree that beliefs around medicine were part of "culture." The terms roughly equated with "culture" in different Malawian languages—*mudauko/midauko* in Chitumbuka and *chikhalidwe/zikhalidwe* in Chichewa—literally translate into English as "the way(s) of living." However, in the context of UNESCO and local initiatives to preserve and promote culture, they had a more restrictive definition that referred to practices more closely associated with ethnic identification and entertainment than with domains of health and ritual. To clarify, in conversations outside the context of efforts at cultural preservation, these same individuals considered Vimbuza to be part of "the way(s) of living." The issue was what kind of cultural practices were appropriate for the type of identity making and exoteric displays resulting from UNESCO-mandated preservation efforts rather than a disagreement about what was or was not "culture."

Healer Lestina Makwakwa echoed this sentiment and was adamant that Vimbuza is a disease that should not be treated as a cultural element. She was especially critical of the idea of a Vimbuza festival, which was part of the safeguarding plan that followed the UNESCO designation, or other events in which Vimbuza would be performed outside of its ritual context, because these displays strip it of its significance. She elaborated that those afflicted with Vimbuza could not entertain because while "dancing" they would not have control over themselves. She gave the example of people being psychotic or entering physically dangerous states, a common occurrence during Vimbuza rituals. In an entertainment context, the possessed person would not be able to start and stop the behavior, and a healer would not be present to oversee the process and ensure the person's safety. Healers Gondwe and Luhanga similarly explained that they felt that these performers were making fun of Vimbuza. They felt that people whose only knowledge of Vimbuza was through these entertainment displays would not take the disease seriously nor respect them for their important work as healers.

In contrast, Healer Mercy Chirwa reacted positively to Vimbuza gaining international recognition. Chirwa explained that it was good for Vimbuza to receive this exposure so that more people would come to understand the disease and the importance of the healing process. I noted that it was the Department of Culture rather than the Department of Health that was promoting Vimbuza, and she responded that Vimbuza should be under the Department of Health. She was less critical than others about Vimbuza being displayed as entertainment because she felt that these positive portrayals helped educate people and bring more understanding both to the problems associated with the disease and the importance of the healing process. In her positive assessment of its promotion as "culture," she thus emphasized health: the more people understood, the more that people would be able to obtain the healing they needed.

Other Malawians I interviewed were critical of the choice of Vimbuza for the UNESCO Representative List because of their own perspectives on religion and medicine. Some did not believe in Vimbuza spirits or that illness could be caused by spirits, so they did not think that the ritual should be encouraged. Others believed that interaction with spirits was tantamount to satanic practices that should be banned, a perspective that I heard repeatedly not only during my more formal interviews but also in informal conversations with students, colleagues, and friends in northern Malawi. Some who were critical of Vimbuza for its problematic medical or religious dimensions supported its recognition as a cultural element meant for entertainment and cultural identity, but only if divorced from spirits and the ritual setting.

When I asked Vimbuza healers if they felt they or Vimbuza had benefited from its UNESCO status, most explained that they perceived very little difference since its inscription. Gondwe and Luhanga, whose Vimbuza temple is now recognized by the government and appears on the map on UNESCO's ICH website, indicated that it was only those practitioners who had been directly "involved with UNESCO" for a long time who had received any benefits. Gondwe and Luhanga had been involved with UNESCO only since the recognition of their temple, two years before I interviewed them. They explained that since the temple's recognition they had attended some UNESCO meetings and events, and a team associated with the UNESCO initiative had come to document their temple. From these activities, they had received some photographs and videotapes, but that was all. They alluded to not having received any material benefit, which tends to be a big emphasis in Malawi, where many people seek material support from those with more resources, especially international organizations. Encouraging them to think beyond money, I pressed them to consider whether there had been any other benefits (for example, social, cultural, or religious), but they could not think of any.

Jejeka Chisusu Mbale, the healer who had been most involved with the UNESCO process, was the most articulate about the benefits to practitioners. Like the others, he emphasized the value of promoting Vimbuza because those afflicted need the appropriate care and treatment. He explained that in addition to being significant for celebrating an important cultural practice, the festivals were important for bringing healers together, building community and sharing knowledge. Unlike those who criticized the festivals for decontextualizing the dance from ritual, he felt that by learning something about Vimbuza, audience members would understand the necessity of preserving this important form. In his valuing of the museum exhibit, Mbale emphasized the controversial issue of witchcraft: the government, churches, and others deny that witchcraft exists, yet it is clearly the cause of great harm in the country. For the exhibit, therefore, they displayed materials used by witches against their victims, much of which is usually hidden from the general public. He hoped that the exhibit would convince people that witchcraft exists and that lawmakers would subsequently overturn the Witchcraft Act, allowing healers to openly identify witches and treat witchcraft-related problems. Mbale also hoped that the government, motivated by the international recognition, would coordinate a meeting between healers and church leaders so that they could come to an understanding that would allow for greater respect for and less condemnation of healers by the churches.

Discussion: From the Local to the National to the International

In a country with a great diversity of cultural identities, belief systems, and lifestyles, selecting two ICH forms to be representative for the country, or even a region or ethnic group, is inherently problematic. Cultural workers overseeing the nomination process understand the impossibility of this task and plan to identify a range of ICH for future nominations; eventually the list should better reflect the diversity in the country, yet it will always be selective.

My interviews raise the question about whether to be ethnically or regionally representative a cultural element should be considered representative by all those in a region or ethnic group. Should Vimbuza not have been inscribed because so many Tumbukas are critical of the ritual and do not participate in it? Or was its inscription appropriate because it is an iconic and widespread phenomenon across the northern region that has religious, medical, and cultural value? It is also significant that neither Vimbuza nor Gule Wamkulu, the other Malawian dance form on the list, are inclusive forms. Gule Wamkulu is exclusive to Chewa men initiated into Nyau, and Vimbuza is primarily danced by those afflicted with spirits. This exclusivity is especially significant now because only two Malawian items have been inscribed. Should more inclusive participatory forms have been deemed "representative" before more esoteric ones?

The UNESCO convention requires involving people at the community level throughout the application process. Nevertheless, the process in Malawi has been top-down. People at the grassroots level have not approached UNESCO with their applications; rather governmental and UNESCO officials approach communities and identify community representatives to participate in the application process, which can result in many people being unaware, ambivalent, or even critical about an inscription. A more grassroots process would involve multiple stakeholders in a community identifying cultural practices that a large percentage of an ethnic group or region considered to be worthy of this status, but even then, the result would be inevitably limited and represent the perspectives of only a percentage of the relevant population.

Preparing a candidature file for UNESCO requires a level of skill and ability quite different from that needed to "safeguard" the practice; to some extent preparation necessitates this top-down approach, as many practitioners do not have access to the knowledge, skills, and resources necessary for completing such a comprehensive file (Kirshenblatt-Gimblett 2004). Furthermore, the process requires that there is adequate information and expertise available. The ironic result in Malawi is that the two selected forms were those still vibrant within their communities and for which there was already lots of information—publications, expertise, museum exhibits, and performances. Creating applications for cultural forms in more critical need of safeguarding or promotion would be far more challenging, time consuming, and expensive.

Who benefits? Few Malawians are aware of Vimbuza's inscription; in fact, few even know that UNESCO or ICH lists exist, and those that do ascribe little value to them. Yet many Malawians, especially adults living in rural areas, are quick to express their concerns about cultural changes taking place. A common criticism is that people are adopting "foreign" ways at the expense of indigenous ones. Many people with whom I have discussed this issue over the past twenty years convey a desire for government-sponsored initiatives aimed at cultural preservation, particularly of those practices related to day-to-day living—demonstrating respect for elders, menarche rituals, courting and marriage customs, and sexual mores—as opposed to the kinds of framed cultural forms that tend to make it to UNESCO lists, that is, those that can more easily be identified, named, and displayed in videos, museum exhibits, and festivals. The Department of Culture is the official Malawian body that oversees the selection and submission of nomination files, and it is also the governmental body charged with promoting culture. After hearing people express their concerns, I asked what they felt the Department of Culture was doing to address their needs: "little to nothing" was the answer, which suggests that many people who are concerned about cultural vitality do not feel the government or UNESCO is addressing their needs.

International critics writing about the 2003 Convention noticed that the lists tend to privilege the colorful and exotic (Smith and

Akagawa 2009). The selection of Vimbuza and Gule Wamkulu in Malawi is striking because both are among the more "colorful" and "exotic" of Malawian dance forms. Many contemporary Malawian dance forms, including Malipenga and Chiwoda in the Rumphi District, are much less "exotic" in that they are secular and feature combinations of European and African idioms and thus reflect the hybridity of contemporary Malawian cultures. The UNESCO list is widely perceived to be an opportunity for enhancing tourism. The hope is that tourists will be drawn to countries with interesting physical and cultural heritage when advertised by such a reputable organization. The nomination of cultural forms by Malawi government and UNESCO officials that correspond to common stereotypes about Africans as primitive may not be intentional; however, the emphasis on these types of cultural forms could reinforce stereotypes about African people rather than provide opportunities for enhanced cross-cultural understanding. Drawing tourist attention to popular hybrid secular dance forms such as Malipenga or Chiwoda could productively educate tourists about the cultural hybridity of contemporary Malawian life and counteract negative stereotypes. On the other hand, the negative stereotyping of African cultural practices as primitive is inherently problematic; providing practitioners with opportunities to share and explain esoteric forms such as Vimbuza and Gule Wamkulu could help to mitigate the disturbing privileging of Western cultural practices as somehow modern and contemporary while African ones are conceived as primitive and backward.

Malawi has limited resources and the cultural sphere has not been considered to be central to development in the myriad of governmental initiatives and projects categorized under the development umbrella. Though not articulated as such, development has largely been a project of Westernization, with the emphasis on developing Western institutions associated with economics, politics, health, and education conceived as necessary for improving life for people in African contexts. Though people on the ground may have little exposure to UNESCO or may not understand its significance, a broader perspective beyond that of practitioners or those in the region reveals some obvious benefits. The limited funding that UNESCO provides through its ICH Convention has supported some important cultural initiatives, and the Convention mandates that the government attend to the cultural sector, resulting in some, albeit limited, developments that probably would not otherwise have occurred. Since the Convention's ratification, the Department of Culture convened an official body, the National Intangible Cultural Heritage Committee, that comprises cultural workers, academics, and ethnic association members, among others, who now meet regularly to share information and strategies. Additionally, the Department of Culture, together with the local UNESCO Commission, has surveyed ICH elements across the country, documenting cultural practices and stimulating greater interest in and awareness of their value. The incentive to submit subsequent candidature files will instigate additional research, and as more elements are added to the list, more activities will be coordinated to promote them.

Though the forms that made it to the list may not represent what a majority of people are most concerned about, they are practices that can easily be documented and displayed in concerts, festivals, and museum exhibits to celebrate cultural identity and diversity. They can also be commoditized and marketed for a tourist audience; they are aesthetically compelling, entertaining, and can be made accessible to outsiders. Integrating these forms into cultural tourism could contribute to sorely needed economic development. The two festivals and the museum exhibit about Vimbuza have increased exposure and education around the practice so that people in Malawi and foreigners have access to more information. Producing exhibits, organizing festivals, and making information accessible online about Vimbuza provides respectful information about a cultural practice that is often vilified and can contribute to greater cross-cultural understanding. The development of a national Vimbuza association will be important for promoting and continuing this cultural practice.[8] From the perspective of the healers interviewed, it is vital that Vimbuza ritual be recognized and protected so that those suffering from spirit-related illnesses can receive the diagnosis and healing they badly need.

The emphasis on community involvement by UNESCO, though problematic because of the impossibility of getting representation from all stakeholders involved in a practice, nevertheless ensures that at least some people "on the ground" are involved. This also increases awareness and the valuing of cultural practices that many otherwise feel are problematic or at least not as important in this "modern world."

Acknowledgments

The research for this essay was funded by a 2012–13 Fulbright US Scholar Grant, a 2010 Research Grant from the University of Oregon's Center for the Study of Women in Society, and a 2010 Summer Research Award from the University of Oregon's Office of Research and Faculty Development.

Notes

1. For more detailed studies of Vimbuza, see Friedson 1996 and Chilivumbo 1972.

2. Another Malawian music/dance form, Gule Wamkulu of the Chewa people, was also first proclaimed on the Masterpieces list and then incorporated onto the Representative List. Malawi, Mozambique, and Tanzania submitted the application for Gule Wamkulu jointly, and the safeguarding efforts are intended to involve regional collaborations between the three countries. Malawi ratified the 2003 Convention for the Safeguarding of Intangible Cultural Heritage in 2010.

3. The Department of Culture, the government entity overseeing cultural initiatives, is regularly moved into different ministries, which it shares with other departments. The configuration at the time of writing in 2013 was the Ministry of Tourism, Wildlife, and Culture, indicative of plans to develop cultural tourism alongside that of wildlife.

4. This list is reproduced as documented in the application. Christopher J. Magomelo, Senior Programme Officer (Culture) of the Malawi National Commission of UNESCO, generously provided me access to the Vimbuza candidature file.

5. See the entry for "Vimbuza healing dance" at http://www.unesco.org/culture /ich/en/RL/00158.

6. The safeguarding project is documented in a leaflet produced by the Malawi National Commission for UNESCO titled "Vimbuza Healing Dance Safeguarding Project 2007–2009."

7. Mbale is unusual for a traditional healer for his level of formal education. He is a retired schoolteacher who speaks English fluently. He explained that he was selected to represent Vimbuza practitioners in the UNESCO process because of his education and English literacy.

8. According to Mbale, the government insisted that the Vimbuza association be national even though the practice is mostly associated with the Tumbuka, an example of the tension that exists between the government's stated objective to promote culture at a national level in a country with so many different cultural groupings.

References Cited

Byrne, Carrie. 2011. "Hunting the Vulnerable: Witchcraft and the Law in Malawi." *Consultancy Africa Intelligence*. http://www.consultancyafrica.com/index .php?option=com_content&view=article&id=783:hunting-the-vulnerable -witchcraft-and-the-law-in-malawi&catid=91:rights-in-focus&Itemid=296.

Chilivumbo, A. B. 1972. "Vimbuza or Mashawe: A Mystic Therapy." *African Music Journal* 5 (2): 6–9.

de Kok, Bregje. 2005. *Christianity and African Traditional Religion: Two Realities of a Different Kind. A Cultural Psychological Study of the Way Christian Malawians Account for Their Involvement in African Traditional Religion.* Zomba, Malawi: Kachere Series.

Friedson, Steven M. 1996. *Dancing Prophets: Musical Experience in Tumbuka Healing.* Chicago: University of Chicago Press.

Gilman, Lisa. 2009. *The Dance of Politics: Gender, Performance, and Democratization in Malawi.* Philadelphia: Temple University Press.

Kirshenblatt-Gimblett, Barbara. 2004. "Intangible Heritage as Metacultural Production." *Museum International* 56 (1–2): 52–65.

Smith, Laurajane, and Natsuko Akagawa. 2009. "Introduction." In *Intangible Heritage,* edited by Laurajane Smith and Natsuko Akagawa, 1–8. New York: Routledge.

Soko, Boston, and Gerhard Kubik. 2008. *Nchimi Chikanga: The Battle against Witchcraft in Malawi.* Zomba, Malawi: Kachere Series.

LISA GILMAN is Associate Professor of Folklore and English at the University of Oregon. She researches dance, gender, and politics in Malawi and has published on the use of women's dancing in Malawi's political sphere. She has also done extensive research with US veterans of the Iraq and Afghanistan conflicts.

4   Imagined UNESCOs: Interpreting Intangible Cultural Heritage on a Japanese Island

TOSHIDON IS A "visiting deity" (*raihōshin*) ritual that takes place every New Year's Eve on a small island off the southwest coast of Japan. Performed for purposes of education, Toshidon is an event in which groups of men, masked and costumed as demon-deity figures, walk from house to house frightening and disciplining children. In 2009, Toshidon was inscribed on the UNESCO Representative List, a significant occurrence for this relatively isolated community. Based on ongoing fieldwork on the island, this essay explores specific events and discourses that emerged from this recognition. I conclude that the UNESCO inscription becomes a floating signifier within the community, one of many elements in an ongoing discussion about the broader future of the island itself.

Location: Shimo-Koshikijima, Kagoshima Prefecture, Japan

Toshidon takes place on the island of Shimo-Koshikijima in Kagoshima Prefecture. Kagoshima is in the southwest of Kyushu, one of the four major islands of Japan. Shimo-Koshikijima is the southernmost of three small islands known collectively as the Koshiki Archipelago (Koshiki rettō). While Kagoshima Prefecture has numerous islands, most are located to the south, between the mainland and the Okinawa region. In contrast, the Koshiki Archipelago is approximately twenty miles off the west coast of the prefecture and therefore somewhat culturally distinct from the mainland and from other islands. Shimo-Koshikijima currently has a total population of 2,459 residents (1,516 households).[1] There is no airport on the island, but a ferry runs daily from the mainland.

The region is temperate with only occasional snowfall, but it is subject to typhoons in late summer and early autumn. Historically, island residents made their living through farming and fishing, but in recent years construction, public works, and civil administration have become the primary industries. Currently, a bridge is being constructed between Shimo-Koshikijima and its neighboring island (Naka-Koshikijima), a project that will keep numerous residents employed in construction and service fields over the next several years and which will eventually alter the relationship between the three islands. Shimo-Koshikijima has several small hotels and bed-and-breakfast accommodations but few other facilities to accommodate visitors; tourism is relatively limited.

In 2004, all three islands merged administratively with the city of Sendai on the mainland to create a new entity called Satsumasendai City. On Shimo-Koshikijima the merger was decided by a close referendum and remains controversial. One ramification was an influx of non-islanders to work in government offices and, inversely, an outflow of island natives to staff administrative facilities in Satsumasendai City. Ultimately, the merger seems to have contributed to a decrease in population on Shimo-Koshikijima, which remains a major problem for the island. While the overall population decreases every year, the percentage of older residents is rapidly growing. Although this trend is common throughout rural communities in the country (Japan is an "aging society"), it is more extreme in peripheral regions such as islands and rural communities where there is little work for younger residents. Shimo-Koshikijima does not have a high school, and it has long been customary for students to finish their education on the mainland. Many find work and establish families there and never return to live on the island.

The Toshidon ritual takes place in six different communities or neighborhoods, each one with its own set of procedures, protocols, and costumes. My own research is based primarily in the hamlet of Teuchi (population approximately 700), where Toshidon is performed in three neighborhoods: Minato, Fumoto, and Motomachi. Fumoto and Motomachi have the highest populations and are generally most active in terms of Toshidon. The description below is based primarily on these two communities, with reference to several others.[2]

ICH Element: Koshikijima no Toshidon

Toshidon is one of a number of rituals found throughout Japan in which masked figures travel from house to house scaring children, often on New Year's Eve or another set date early in the new year.[3] The word *Toshidon* refers to both the ritual itself as well as the masked demon-deities. In Fumoto and Motomachi, it is said that on December 31, the last night of the old year, the Toshidon will descend from the "skyworld" (*tenjōkai*) to visit the children of the community, to scold them for their bad behavior throughout the year and to reward them for what they have done well. It is a terrifying rite of passage for the children and a much-anticipated event for the family.

At around six in the evening, while families are preparing at home, men gather at the community center to transform themselves into Toshidon. They help each other dress in costumes made of straw, *sotetsu* palm fronds, and other local plant materials, and they don colorful, oversized cardboard masks with extremely long noses. In groups of four or five, with an entourage of noise-making companions, they walk through the dark night to households where families are gathered. At each house, they rattle *shoji* screens, thump on walls, roar threateningly, and finally enter on their hands and knees, like wild creatures. Once inside, they face the children one by one, making each child stand and recite her name. They scold her for bad behavior—not cleaning up toys, for example, or not eating vegetables—and praise her for good behavior, such as doing her homework or being kind to her younger brother. Then they command the child to sing a song she learned in school. Next, she is challenged to touch a Toshidon's nose, to make contact, literally, with this messenger from the otherworld. Finally, after promising to behave properly during the coming year, she is given a reward—a huge *mochi* rice cake—which she receives by crawling backward toward the Toshidon, who place the rice cake on her back. The Toshidon only spend about twenty minutes in each household, but for children it is an unforgettable encounter, a test of courage fraught with quavering voices and tears—and boasted about with pride the next day.

Costumes, masks, and procedures vary with each neighborhood, but most residents agree that all versions of Toshidon share the

FIGURE 1
Toshidon enter a house in Motomachi on New Year's Eve, 2011. Photograph by author.

objective of "disciplining" children, generally between the ages of four and eight. The disciplinary focus is explicit: in most neighborhoods, families wishing to participate submit a form to the community center on which they list specific points for which they would like each of their children to be scolded or praised. The event itself is a complexly choreographed and improvised physical performance in which the Toshidon, children, and family members enact roles within a broader community structure. Islanders have explained to me that the dialogue between Toshidon and child, often including interactions with parents and other family members, is critical to the success of the "happening."[4] Indeed, the instruction and support provided by parents during the performance is considered important for nurturing appropriate connections within the family and within the broader community.

Beyond the ritual moment itself, Toshidon plays a role in local life throughout the year. Parents remind children that the Toshidon live in the "skyworld," where they are always looking down and making note of their behavior. That is, most of the year they are invisible—existing only as hearsay and memory—making their New Year's Eve appearance all the more powerful. One six-year old girl told me that Toshidon had scolded her friend for playing with matches earlier in the year. "It's *true*," she said with awe. "There was nobody else there, but Toshidon-sama saw it!"[5]

There is no documented evidence attesting to when the tradition began but it is likely that it has taken place in one way or another for at least 130 years and probably much longer. Current residents in their eighties and nineties remember their parents talking about their own experiences receiving Toshidon, and the ritual was also imported to another island, Tanegashima (where it is still performed), by migrants from Shimo-Koshikijima in the 1880s. Many islanders explain that in the past Toshidon was enacted by junior high school boys and other young men, but today the performers, while still only male, are usually at least in their twenties and sometimes significantly older. In the past so many families received visitations from Toshidon that each neighborhood would require several groups to make the rounds; with the decrease in population in recent years, however, only a few families in each neighborhood have a child of appropriate age. Moreover, since involvement in the ritual is entirely voluntary, some families may choose not to be involved (for any number of reasons), further decreasing the number of participating children.

While Toshidon has experienced periods of great liveliness as well as decline, for the past several decades islanders have self-consciously celebrated it as an important cultural asset. In 1977 the Japanese Agency for Cultural Affairs (Bunkachō) selected "Koshikijima no Toshidon" [Toshidon of Koshiki Island] as one of the first "important intangible folk cultural properties" (*Jūyō mukei minzoku bunkazai*) in the nation.[6] This recognition came about during a time when small communities throughout Japan were revitalizing and revaluing their local traditions, and the national government was implementing systems of recognition for traditional cultural products, both tangible and intangible (the Japanese infrastructure greatly influenced the development of these mechanisms within UNESCO). In the 1970s, several island leaders—teachers and village employees—actively worked to get Toshidon recognized on a national level. It was this national-level recognition that would eventually lead to its nomination for UNESCO inscription some three decades later.

Current Status with Regard to UNESCO:
One of the "First Elements" in Japan

Of the seventy-six "first elements" inscribed into the Representative List by UNESCO's ICH Committee in September 2009, thirteen were from Japan, including Koshikijima no Toshidon.[7] The nomination submitted (in English) to UNESCO reads:

> They have a common faith that a deity of a peculiar appearance, called Toshidon, visits the human world on the night of December 31. This simple and innocent faith has sustained the Toshidon practice on Shimo-Koshikijima as an annual event, transmitted from generation to generation up to the present time, and thus it is recognized as part of their cultural heritage collectively transmitted by the community. (UNESCO 2009)

The nomination was not submitted to UNESCO by the islanders but by the Japanese national government. Because Toshidon had been one of the earliest "important intangible folk cultural properties" on a national level, the Japanese Agency for Cultural Affairs simply sought the approval of local residents and then proceeded to nominate it. Village officials told me that they had the feeling that, as far as the Agency for Cultural Affairs was concerned, it was simply Toshidon's "turn" to be nominated.[8] Other than signing off on the nomination form, the islanders themselves had no direct involvement with the UNESCO selection; in fact, they only realized the inscription was official when a newspaper reporter from the mainland called the village office to ask how they felt about it. It was not until spring of the following year (2010) that they received an official certificate; the original (in English) and a Japanese translation are now displayed in the small history museum in Teuchi.

On-the-Ground Perspectives:
Excitement, Concern, Discussion

The UNESCO selection was a big deal on the island: residents were thrilled and "surprised" (*bikkuri*). One community leader told a mainland newspaper, "It is wonderful that the world knows about this event on an isolated island in the corner of Japan" (*Minami Nippon shinbun* 2009). There were a number of immediate tangible responses to the recognition. First there were signs, literally: banners celebrating the designation were displayed, two on the façade of the town hall and one at the ferry terminal in Teuchi. Posters were placed in various public spaces, such as the town hall and neighborhood community centers. In November, the village office invited Professor Shimono Toshimi, a leading authority on the folklore of southern Japan, to lecture on Toshidon. The talk was attended by about 150 people, an impressive showing for an island of this size.[9] Shimono discussed the known history of the ritual and also predicted that because of the UNESCO designation hundreds of tourists might come to see Toshidon in the years to come. Finally, for that New Year's Eve (2009), Satsumasendai City commissioned a professional film crew to document the Toshidon performance in all six neighborhoods. The goal was to create a DVD of the events on this particular day, the first performance after the UNESCO inscription. The resulting DVD was not to be sold but simply kept as a record (*kiroku*) in the city administrative offices.[10]

The decision to film Toshidon was notable because, at least since the 1970s, different neighborhoods have had distinct attitudes toward filming and photographing, or even toward allowing tourists to witness Toshidon. In particular, residents of Fumoto have generally prohibited photographs of the ritual and directed inquiries from television and film crews elsewhere. Various reasons are proffered for this ban, but the rationale is, in part, that outside visitors (especially with cameras and flashes) would distract participants, destroy the atmosphere, and attenuate the intensity of the ritual. In contrast, the Motomachi neighborhood has been open to outside attention and, within limits, welcomes photographers, film crews, and tourists.[11] So while the decision to film in all six neighborhoods in 2009 was indicative of how momentous UNESCO recognition was felt to be, it was also significant that the DVD would not be used for commercial purposes or shown on television.[12]

While these were the concrete ramifications of UNESCO recognition, there have also been more abstract and affective responses. For the most part, islanders have embraced the designation as a point of pride: it is mentioned in advertising brochures and public events and the certificate itself is displayed. At the same time, however, many islanders voice concern that UNESCO recognition will cause the performance of Toshidon to stagnate. They argue that the ritual was always "informal" and "personal": you would just ask a neighbor or friend to dress up in a scary fashion "with whatever was at hand"

and come scold and praise your children. Masks, costumes, and procedures were flexible and reinvented each year—a tactical response to the needs of the moment. Some islanders fear that the UNESCO designation will freeze Toshidon at this particular juncture in its history, and the images recorded on the DVD will become the reference for future performances.[13] At this moment of global recognition, they stress, it is particularly critical to remember that flexibility has always been part of the tradition.

Similarly, even before UNESCO recognition became official, there were concerns about losing autonomy and control of Toshidon. One local leader told me that when he first heard that the Agency for Cultural Affairs might nominate Toshidon to UNESCO, he feared they would be forced to adhere to outside standards or change their performance in some way. Only after assurance from Satsumasendai City officials that this was not the case, that UNESCO would have no control over the performance itself, did he sign off on the nomination.

This same leader, however, went on to explain that despite the fact that UNESCO has indeed been completely "hands off," he and others have "internalized" the recognition and feel a certain "burden" because of Toshidon's newfound global status. This "burden" does not extend to how the ritual is actually performed but is manifest as an increased sense of responsibility for the future of the tradition. Since Toshidon is child-oriented and there are fewer and fewer children on the island, it is possible that in years to come they will not be able to perform it regularly, if at all. While they do not want to transform Toshidon into a performance spectacle (*misemono*), some residents feel UNESCO recognition compels them to keep the tradition alive in some form.

The future of Toshidon is something the islanders have been grappling with for a long time, but UNESCO and the intangible sense of responsibility it inspires make this dilemma all the more urgent. The inscription becomes part of a general discussion about the island's wellbeing, inspiring residents to more deeply consider Toshidon's role in a community facing a startling decline in youth population. In 2012 there were only 122 elementary school children on the entire island.[14] In the Motomachi neighborhood, Toshidon visited four households in 2011, five in 2012, and three in 2013; leaders have calculated that, given current family situations, there may be no children of appropriate age left within the next three or four years. What then happens to Toshidon? Most people I spoke with insisted that if there are no longer any children, Toshidon would and *should* disappear. It should not, they asserted, persist only as a tourist attraction.

But in practice Toshidon's inscription on the Representative List is entwined with discussions of tourism. As mentioned above, folklorist Shimono Toshimi predicted a massive increase in tourists—a prediction that was not taken seriously by everybody but was, nevertheless, widely discussed. Although there is a municipal tourist board on the island, all decisions concerning Toshidon and tourism are made by the six neighborhood Toshidon *hozonkai* or "preservation societies." Each society, consisting of four or five members, is responsible for organizing the ritual every year and for thinking through the longer-term issues associated with its performance and, as the name implies, "preservation."

Both the Fumoto and Motomachi preservation societies face the same issues of depopulation, but their responses with regard to tourism have been markedly different. In Fumoto, where photography has long been forbidden, the approach has been relatively straightforward: despite greater pressure to open up to television crews and others, the society remains firm about *not* performing Toshidon for tourists. This notorious ban effectively limits tourist involvement and at the same time gives the Fumoto version an aura of "authenticity," as the thing hidden from sight becomes all the more desired.

In Motomachi, where residents have always been relatively open to visitors, the response has been more complex. As soon as it was suspected that UNESCO would recognize Toshidon, the preservation society began discussions about whether or not they should "open up" the ritual. In the society leader's words, "very strong opinions" were expressed on both sides. Those against "opening up" argued that "children would not focus on Toshidon but on the camera: their concentration would scatter . . . and the original meaning of Toshidon would be lost." They claimed that the "ritual takes place in the family household" and "should not become a spectacle." On the opposing side it was argued that outsiders "would come to understand the importance of Toshidon," that "it was necessary to share it with the public" and that it might be an "important form of local [economic] revitalization."[15]

The Motomachi preservation society was conscious of treading a delicate line between inclusivity and the maintenance of what it considered the integrity and effectiveness of Toshidon; in the end, they decided to open the ritual on a limited basis—so that visitors might be accommodated but events would not be disrupted. In 2008, the year before the official UNESCO inscription, they began advertising and accepting applications. Significantly, they did not seek "tourists" (*kankōkyaku*) but specifically called for *kengakusha*, a word that can be translated as "visitor" or "observer" but which is constructed from the characters for "see" and "learn," and suggests a purpose beyond mere pleasure or sightseeing. "Unless they have an intense interest," the head of the society explained to me, "nobody is going to make the effort to come all the way to this isolated island on the margins of the country just to see Toshidon."[16]

Still, the preservation society realized that by opening Toshidon to visitors, they risked changing its value for the families and children to whom it was directed. They took strict precautions, refusing commercial tour groups and limiting the number of kengakusha to twenty, a size that might reasonably observe the ritual from inside individual households. The advertising flyer included a sober warning that "the ritual takes place in private households so all kengakusha must follow the guidance of the people in charge."

In practice, preservation society members carefully orchestrate visitors' experiences. At seven o'clock in the evening, kengakusha are welcomed at the community hall and provided with a brief description of Toshidon that emphasizes its educational function. They are then led to several houses, where they are ushered, quietly, to good vantage points inside. Photography is allowed in some houses and forbidden in others, depending on the preferences of the particular family. About an hour later, after the Toshidon have made their rounds and the ritual is complete, visitors are led back to the community hall for discussion with participants, facilitated by beer and sweet potato *shōchū*, the alcohol of choice on the island. Most visitors return to the mainland the following day, the first of January.[17]

Discussion: Depopulation, Tourism, and the Future of the Island

I have argued elsewhere (Foster 2011) that one effect of the UNESCO designation is *defamiliarization*: the fact that a global body had taken note of Toshidon and added it to a list of similarly important examples of intangible cultural heritage around the world makes islanders step back and view their own tradition from a different perspective. UNESCO contributes an outside voice and added intensity to discussions of depopulation, employment, transportation infrastructure, and tourism development. During debates in the Satsumasendai City council, for example, Eguchi Konohiko, the representative from the islands, reminds other councilors that they should remember Toshidon's UNESCO designation when considering economic and administrative policies.

Certainly, being singled out by UNESCO has reinforced Toshidon's position within a broader discourse about the past, present, and future of the island, but the designation is by no means a deciding factor in this discourse. Nor has it really affected the day-to-day lives of the islanders. Even as tourism is embraced by the Motomachi preservation society, other neighborhoods tend to get few outside visitors.[18] In fact, tourists face numerous obstacles: ferries are frequently cancelled due to inclement weather, the largest hotel in Teuchi only has fourteen guestrooms, and the few shops and restaurants on the island are closed over the New Year's holidays.

Even in Motomachi, experiences over the last few years only illustrate ongoing challenges for both visitor and host. In 2009, the year of the designation and concomitant media attention, nineteen people preregistered to visit, but ferries were canceled because of rough weather on December 31. As a result, only nine tourists, who had made the crossing the day before, witnessed the event. In 2010, a winter storm caused ferries to be cancelled for two consecutive days and not a single tourist arrived in time. In 2011 the weather held and there were twelve kengakusha, and in 2012 there were fourteen. In 2013 the weather was excellent, but because the Toshidon were only visiting three houses that year, the Motomachi Preservation Society decided this would not provide an interesting experience and did not formally invite kengakusha. Instead, a professional photographer and several film crews (a documentary filmmaker and a local Kagoshima television station) were the only outside visitors.

Ultimately the event itself may not bring many tourists at all; there are places much more accessible for domestic tourists with only a few days off over the New Year's holidays. At the same time, however, the head of the island tourist board suggested to me that the *fact* of Toshidon—and its heralded association with UNESCO—is valuable in branding the island as a unique destination, regardless of whether one actually gets a chance to see the ritual itself. In this context, UNESCO is a powerful brand; many people in Japan have long been keenly interested in "world heritage sites" (*sekai-isan*)—the tangible kind, that is. Moreover, nationally designated ICHs have been part of domestic tourist consciousness for decades. So the fact that Shimo-Koshikijima has a UNESCO-designated ICH—regardless of whether one gets to see it or not—makes great advertising copy for the island, for Satsumasendai City, and for Kagoshima Prefecture.[19] Having said this, however, there is also a disconnect between islanders' perceptions of the importance of UNESCO recognition and the understanding of Toshidon off the island. Despite national media coverage of Toshidon's inscription, very few people in Japan (outside the folkloric community) have actually heard of Toshidon. Even a Buddhist priest born and bred in Kushikino, the small port city where the ferry leaves for Shimo-Koshikijima, told me he had only vaguely heard of it.

At the same time, my impression is that islanders feel—or want to feel—that Toshidon is known throughout the country. This was brought home to me when, after several months living on the island, I was asked by the preservation societies to give a public lecture about my research. Rather than discuss Toshidon itself, I felt I could be more helpful by talking about UNESCO and ICH generally. With the intention of putting Toshidon's selection into a broader context, I showed slides of the twelve other ICHs from Japan selected in 2009. Most of these traditions from disparate parts of the country are very local and, unsurprisingly, almost completely unknown to the islanders. The only really famous element on the list is "Yamahoko, the float ceremony of the Kyoto Gion festival," part of a grand summer event that receives tens of thousands of visitors each year.[20] I expected the islanders to be disappointed by the list, concluding that just as they had never heard of most of these other ICHs, perhaps people elsewhere had never heard of Toshidon. Several islanders did indeed respond to the list I presented, but to my surprise it was not because they had never heard of the other traditions: rather, they were excited to learn that UNESCO had put Toshidon on par with a festival as famous as Gion in Kyoto.

I hesitate to generalize here, but at least to some islanders, Toshidon's inscription elevates it into exclusive company, placing it into both a national and global "heritage-scape" (Di Giovine 2009) with similarly distinguished traditions.[21] One island friend described the selection not as a point of "pride" but rather as a reason for "confidence" or *jishin*. I have written of this before (Foster 2011), but the characterization continues to ring true. The word *jishin* might be literally translated as "self belief," and implies a deep sense that what one is doing has meaning. My friend explained that the UNESCO designation may be a label imposed by distant authorities, but it confirmed what he already felt: that Toshidon is a meaningful tradition. UNESCO provided what he saw as an objective confirmation of his own subjective values.

In the final analysis, the only conclusion I can draw at this stage is that the effect of UNESCO and the ICH designation on the ground in Shimo-Koshikijima is varied, complex, and emerging. For many people UNESCO is seen as performing a kind of critical gaze, reminding islanders of a world outside the island and at the same time, because of its semiotic openness, serving as a mutable element within local discussions. Ultimately, it is the malleability and open-endedness of the term that is most striking. *UNESCO* (or *Yunesuko* in Japanese) is a floating signifier open to multiple and conflicting interpretations, imbued with different meanings by different actors in different discursive contexts. Despite UNESCO's existence as a real organization—with employees, a budget, and a brick-and-mortar headquarters in Paris—what it refers to on the island varies from person to person. To some it is a sign of global standing, or inspiration for local pride, or a reason for confidence; to others it is a catalyst for tourism, or a way to leverage municipal funding, or a burden to shoulder for future generations. That is, there are many different UNESCOs, and all of them are, as it were, imagined. For better or for worse, islanders realize that UNESCO recognition cannot be undone; it is up to them to make it their own, to interpret it to their advantage, and to wield it with tactical flexibility as they negotiate the realities and future of life on a small island in contemporary Japan.

Notes

1. All population statistics are from December 1, 2014 (Satsumasendai-shi, http://www.city.satsumasendai.lg.jp/www/contents/1300087101977/index.html).

2. I have been researching Toshidon since 1999 and have observed the ritual in 1999, 2000, 2009, 2011, 2012, and 2013. I have also conducted fieldwork on the island at other times of the year and was in fulltime residence from December 2011 to May 2012; I am grateful for the generous support of a Fulbright Fellowship that funded my research during that period. My descriptions here are based

primarily on the ritual as performed in the neighborhoods of Fumoto and Moto-machi and on numerous formal and informal interviews with island residents as well as visitors. I am profoundly grateful to my friends in these communities for generously putting up with me, and my questions, for so many years. For a more detailed discussion of the ritual and its touristic context, see Foster 2011 and 2013. See also Tsuchiya 2014a and 2014b. Please note: throughout this essay Japanese proper names are written in Japanese order, with family name first. All translations from Japanese, whether oral or written, are my own.

3. In the Ryūkyū island area in the south of Japan, similar observances take place during late summer.

4. Interview with island resident (O. Y.) conducted in January 2000.

5. The suffix -sama is an honorific attached to names and titles of people and gods to show respect. It is commonly used by islanders when speaking of Toshidon.

6. As of June 2015, there were 290 designated important intangible folk cultural properties in Japan, including 7 from Kagoshima Prefecture. See http://kunishitei.bunka.go.jp/bsys/categorylist.asp. For more on intangible cultural properties and preservation law in Japan, see Ōshima 2007; Thornbury 1993, 1994, 1995, 1997, 55–74; Hashimoto 1998, 2003; Cang 2007; and Aikawa-Faure 2014. Japanese cultural properties policies influenced the development of UNESCO's ICH conceptions and programs (Kurin 2004, 67–68). Moreover the Masterpieces Program and the 2003 ICH Convention were both formalized by UNESCO while Kōichirō Matsuura, a Japanese diplomat, was serving as Director-General.

7. The elements added in 2009 are Akiu no Taue Odori; Chakkirako; Daimokutate; Dainichido Bugaku; Gagaku; Hayachine Kagura; Hitachi Furyumono; Koshikijima no Toshidon; Ojiya-chijimi, Echigo-jofu; Oku-noto no Aenokoto; Sekishu-Banshi; Traditional Ainu Dance; and Yamahoko, the float ceremony of the Kyoto Gion festival. (I render them here the way they are translated and transliterated in the UNESCO list itself; see http://www.unesco.org/culture/ich/index.php?pg=00011).

8. This seems to be a fairly accurate characterization of the process at the time. More recently, however, the Agency for Cultural Affairs has started to exercise greater selectivity in its nomination process.

9. There is some dispute as to how many people actually attended the lecture; some people claim there were no more than one hundred attendees while other say there were almost two hundred. Either number attests to significant interest.

10. For more on the visual documentation of tradition in Japan, see Hyōki Satoru 2007.

11. For more on the reasons for these distinctions, see Foster 2011.

12. In May 2012, I attended a joint meeting of the Toshidon Preservation Societies in which members chose to deny a request made by a local television station to broadcast the DVD publically.

13. This may have happened to a certain extent with the 1977 recognition by the Agency for Cultural Affairs; a film made at that time is sometimes used as a reference source.

14. The extent of the decline can be seen in records from Teuchi Primary School: in 1948 there were 667 students; in 2012 only 55 students.

15. I was not present at the meetings where these issues were discussed but am grateful to the head of the Motomachi preservation society, quoted here, for recounting them to me. Interview with U. K., January 2012.

16. Interview with U. K., January 2012.

17. The description here is based on participant observation in 2011, 2012, and 2013.

18. In 2012, for example, when I attended the Toshidon event in the Aose neighborhood, I was the only nonresident present.

19. Toshidon is notably the only UNESCO-recognized ICH in Kagoshima Prefecture, or indeed, within all of Kyushu. The notion of World Heritage is very popular in Japan; the phrase *sekai-isan* is known even by elementary school children (Sataki 2009, 4), and there are numerous television shows documenting visits to heritage sites throughout the world. The inscription of Mount Fuji onto UNESCO's World Heritage List of cultural properties ("Fujisan, sacred place and source of artistic inspiration") was national news in 2013, inspiring major public discussions of UNESCO and tourism. The subsequent inscription in late 2013 of Washoku, or Japanese food, onto the ICH Representative List also made headlines but seemed of less immediate interest to the media; this may be in part because of uncertainty of what recognition of a "national" element entails.

20. In 2013, for example, an estimated 140,000 people lined the streets to witness the procession of floats. In comparison to Toshidon, almost no mention of the festival's UNESCO status is made—presumably because it is simply not needed to drum up tourist interest.

21. For discussion of the power and importance of lists, see Kirshenblatt-Gimblett 2004 and Hafstein 2009.

References Cited

Aikawa-Faure, Noriko. 2014. "Excellence and Authenticity: 'Living National (Human) Treasures' in Japan and Korea." *International Journal of Intangible Heritage* 9:38–51.

Cang, Voltaire Garces. 2007. "Defining Intangible Cultural Heritage and Its Stakeholders: The Case of Japan." *International Journal of Intangible Heritage* 2:46–55.

Di Giovine, Michael A. 2009. *The Heritage-Scape: UNESCO, World Heritage, and Tourism.* Lanham, MD: Rowman and Littlefield.

Foster, Michael Dylan. 2011. "The UNESCO Effect: Confidence, Defamiliarization, and a New Element in the Discourse on a Japanese Island." *Journal of Folklore Research* 48 (1): 63–107.

———. 2013. "Shikakuteki sōzō: 'Koshikijima no Toshidon' ni okeru miru/mirareru kankei no ichi kōsatsu" [The optic imaginary: Thoughts on the relationship of seeing and being seen in 'Koshikijima no Toshidon']. *Nihon minzokugaku* 273:55–95.

Hafstein, Valdimar Tr. 2009. "Intangible Heritage as a List: From the Masterpieces to Representation." In *Intangible Heritage*, edited by Laurajane Smith and Natsuko Akagawa, 93–111. New York: Routledge.

Hashimoto Hiroyuki. 1998. "Re-creating and Re-imagining Folk Performing Arts in Contemporary Japan." *Journal of Folklore Research* 35 (1): 35–46.

————. 2003. "Between Preservation and Tourism: Folk Performing Arts in Contemporary Japan." *Asian Folklore Studies* 62:223–34.

Hyōki Satoru. 2007. "Mukei minzoku bunkazai eizō kiroku no yūkō na hozon, katsuyō no tame no teigen: Jōhō no kyōyū to hirakareta riyō no jitsugen ni mukete" [Proposal for effective preservation and application of visual records of intangible cultural heritage: Toward the realization of information sharing and open use]. *Mukei bunka isan kenkyū hōkoku* 1:41–50.

Kirshenblatt-Gimblett, Barbara. 2004. "Intangible Heritage as Metacultural Production." *Museum International* 56 (1–2): 52–65.

Kurin, Richard. 2004. "Safeguarding Intangible Cultural Heritage in the 2003 UNESCO Convention: A Critical Appraisal." *Museum International* 56 (1–2): 66–77.

Minami Nippon shinbun. 2009. "Yunesuko no mukei bunka isan 'Koshikijima no Toshidon' tōroku" [The inscription of 'Koshikijima no Toshidon' as UNESCO intangible cultural heritage]. October 1.

Ōshima Akio. 2007. *Mukei minzoku bunkazai no hogo: Mukei bunka isan hogo jōyaku ni mukete* [The preservation of intangible folk cultural properties: Toward the Intangible Cultural Heritage Convention]. Tokyo: Iwata shoin.

Sataki Yoshihiro. 2009. *'Sekai isan' no shinjitsu: Kajō na kitai, ōinaru gokai* [The truth of 'World Heritage': Excess expectations, great misunderstandings]. Tokyo: Shōdensha.

Thornbury, Barbara E. 1993. "Festival Setting to Center Stage: Preserving Japan's Folk Performing Arts." *Asian Theater Journal* 10 (2): 163–78.

————. 1994. "The Cultural Properties Protection Law and Japan's Folk Performing Arts." *Asian Folklore Studies* 53 (2): 211–25.

————. 1995. "Folklorism and Japan's Folk Performing Arts." *Journal of Folklore Research* 32 (3): 207–20.

————. 1997. *The Folk Performing Arts: Traditional Culture in Contemporary Japan.* Albany: SUNY Press.

Tsuchiya Hisashi. 2014a. "Shima no seishin bunkashi Dai 19 wa: Toshidon (zen-pen)" [Spiritual-cultural record of an island, number 19: Toshidon (part one)]. *Shima* 237:80–95.

————. 2014b "Shima no seishin bunkashi Dai 20 wa: Toshidon (chūhen)" [Spiritual-cultural record of an island, number 20: Toshidon (part two)] *Shima* 238:94–109.

UNESCO. 2009. "Nomination for Inscription on the Representative List in 2009 (Reference No. 00270)." Convention for the Safeguarding of the Intangible Cultural Heritage Intergovernmental Committee for the Safeguarding of the Intangible Cultural Heritage. Fourth session, Abu Dhabi, United Arab Emirates. September 28 to October 2. http://www.unesco.org/culture/ich/doc/download.php?versionID=30053.

MICHAEL DYLAN FOSTER is Associate Professor of Folklore and East Asian Studies at Indiana University. He is the author of *Pandemonium and Parade: Japanese Monsters and the Culture of Yōkai* (2009), *The Book of Yōkai: Mysterious Creatures of Japanese Folklore* (2015), and numerous articles on Japanese folklore, literature, and media.

5   Macedonia, UNESCO, and Intangible Cultural Heritage: The Challenging Fate of Teškoto

IN MACEDONIA DEBATES about heritage are played out along the fault lines of ethnic and religious conflict as well as a faltering economy and threats from neighbors about interpretations of history. The country's 2002 and 2004 failed applications for a UNESCO Masterpiece of Intangible Cultural Heritage and its ongoing submissions of representative lists provide a valuable case study of how rural folklore symbols are selectively adopted into heritage discourse and elevated to iconic status. This essay analyzes Teškoto (the Heavy/Difficult Dance) as featured in two UNESCO Masterpiece applications as well as in village contexts, ensemble performances, an annual staged ritual, and tourist appropriations. The story of how Teškoto became a national symbol but failed to achieve UNESCO status as ICH illuminates the manner in which nationalist discourse shapes performance practices.

Location: Macedonia

Macedonia, or more properly the Former Yugoslav Republic of Macedonia (FYROM), is a new Balkan state, independent since 1991 (figure 1). Although Macedonia avoided the direct Yugoslav warfare of the 1990s, it has suffered economically due to regional crises and several embargoes imposed by Greece. FYROM and Greece are currently engaged in a legal and political battle over the name Macedonia, which is also the name of a province of Greece. Greece has refused to let FYROM use the name, claiming it has an exclusive tie to ancient Macedonia, ruled by Alexander the Great. Macedonia has countered with its own proofs of antiquity, as embodied in archeological sites and revisionist histories. This battle has been very damaging to Macedonia's development agenda and has also encouraged nationalist

93

FIGURE 1
Map of Macedonia. "The Former Yugoslav Republic of Macedonia,"
no. 3789, rev. 5, August 2007. United Nations, Department of Field Support,
Cartographic Section.

fervor. One manifestation of this fervor is Skopje 2104, an urban
development project in the capital consisting of twenty new buildings
and more than forty new monuments to historical figures; the cost is
over five hundred million euros. The project's centerpiece is an eighty-
foot statue/fountain of Alexander the Great on his horse (figure 2).

Incipient Macedonian nationalism, of course, began long before
the name dispute with Greece. Historical narratives have centered
around the fight for liberation from the Ottoman Empire that ruled
Macedonia for five hundred years, until 1912 (Brown 2003; Neofotistos 2012). Byzantine civilization, the Eastern Orthodox religion, and
village folklore have been glorified as bulwarks of ethnicity against
Muslim invaders. The Turks are often depicted as tyrannical over-
lords, as "the Turkish Yoke," although Western historians paint a
more nuanced picture (Hupchick 1994); many Macedonians view the
Muslim religion as somehow foreign, even though up to 35 percent of
the country is Muslim. The bloody Balkan Wars (1912–13) followed

FIGURE 2
Alexander the Great statue/fountain in the center of Skopje.
Photograph by author.

Macedonia's liberation from the Ottoman Empire, in which Serbia, Bulgaria, and Greece fought over control of Macedonia. Macedonia has thus had a conflictive relationship not only with Greece and Serbia but also with Bulgaria, and many Bulgarians claim there is no such thing as a separate Macedonian ethnicity.

After the victory of the Partisans/socialists in World War II, the Yugoslav government promoted the institutionalization of Macedonian identity and declared Macedonia a constituent "nation" (*narod*); its language was standardized, its history was codified, and its folklore became a central concern of cultural and arts policy. The government valorized ethnic Macedonian folklore, not the folklore of minorities (Seeman 2012). According to Marxist and Leninist principles, promoting art and nation building were entwined: the modernization of society required the creation of new cultural forms such as folk music and dance ensembles. In addition, the government supported KUDs (*Kulturno Umetničko Društvo*)—voluntary organizations of amateur folk artists (Hofman 2008).

In 1949 Tanec, the Macedonian State Ensemble of Folk Dances and Songs, was founded, and folklore collection and preservation efforts escalated. Tanec has been called a "museum in motion," a "three-dimensional presentation of a knowledge long lost" (Tatarchevska 2011, 78). In an insightful article, Macedonian folklorist Ivona Opetcheska Tatarchevska (2011, 79) explicates how folk dance was ideologically tied to nationalism; dance was seen as the "keeper" of "national history." She cites Manoil Čučkov, the first director of Tanec, who wrote that Macedonian folk dances are "the carriers of the new historical contents and a reflection of the socio-political elements of the whole nation"; he further linked dance with national struggle (80). In a sense, Čučkov advocated that dance should provide a historical narrative.

Nation building entered a new phase after Macedonia gained independence in 1991, with ethnic politics taking center stage. According to the most recent Macedonian census (2002), the ethnic populations of Macedonia include Macedonians (64.2 percent of the population), Albanians (25.2 percent), Turks (3.9 percent), and Roma (2.7 percent); some Muslims claim they make up as much as 35 percent of the population.[1] The main conflict that dominates contemporary Macedonian politics is over minority rights: Macedonians fear Albanian secession, Muslim fanaticism, and the loss of Macedonian national identity, and Albanians fear Macedonian suppression of their rights (Neofotistos 2012). The conflict has turned violent several times but is now simmering. In sum, Macedonian ethnic identity is historically fragile; a sense of being besieged externally by neighbors and internally by minorities informs nationalist discourse. Heritage policy is directly affected by this framework.

ICH Element: Teškoto

How did Teškoto become a national ethnic symbol and a proposed ICH element for UNESCO? Teškoto is a men's dance that was performed in the western Macedonian mountainous region of Reka, in the villages of Galičnik, Lazaropolje, and Gari, among others. The inhabitants of this region, who speak a distinct dialect of Macedonian, are known as Mijaks. The majority are Eastern Orthodox; however there were and still are Torbeši (Macedonian-speaking Muslims) who dance Teškoto. Mijaks and Torbeši engaged in agriculture and herding, like other Macedonian villagers, but the males were especially known for their seasonal migratory patterns that took them to Ottoman territories and Europe to find work as stonemasons and other artisans.

Teškoto is a very striking line dance in which the leader displays improvisatory skills. It begins with a dramatic, slow, and nonmetric section where the dancers execute precise lifts, steps, and leaps. The musicians must expertly follow the leader, picking up on visual embodied cues. The music builds in tempo, ending in a fast 2/4 section. The pioneering dance researchers Ljubica and Danica Janković (1934) published a description from Lazaropolje that emphasized the leader's improvisation and squats and turns. In the 1980s Balkan dance ethnographer Elsie Dunin interviewed elderly dancers from the region who stressed: "The dance depended on the leader who was critically judged for his improvisational skill . . . that took great strength and coordination to perform. In Lazaropolje, a dance leader paid for the privilege of leading the dance and he would not relinquish his leadership" (Višinski and Dunin 1995, 263).

Traditionally, Albanian-speaking Muslim Roma (Gypsies) from the city of Debar, near the Albanian border, perform the music that accompanies Teškoto. Roma in Macedonia have very low status in every economic, political, and social niche except music, where they are valued.[2] The Majovci clan of Roma from Debar have performed for Mijak villagers in a patron-client relationship for centuries. The instruments used are *zurla* (a double reed pipe, played in pairs, melody and drone) and *tapan* (a two-headed drum); until recently, Roma had a monopoly on these loud outdoor instruments. Romani professional performers intimately know the entire regional dance repertoire.

Teškoto became a signature dance of Tanec soon after the ensemble was formed. Dunin reports that in the 1940s several dancers from Lazaropolje moved to Skopje and joined the Kočo Racin amateur ensemble and other groups. Many Kočo Racin dancers were accepted into Tanec; in addition, the first dance director of Tanec, Rafe Žikoski, was from Lazaropolje (Višinski and Dunin 1995, 263).[3] Thus, the Lazaropolje connection helped cement Teškoto's role in Tanec.

The traditional contexts for dancing Teškoto are not mentioned by researchers, which leads me to assume that it had no special ritual meaning but was part of the men's dance repertoire for typical village celebrations such as weddings, saints' days, and gatherings after church. Ideologically, however, the dance was endowed with nationalist sentiment during the crucial postwar identity-building period. Tatarchevska (2011, 82) traces the relationship of Teškoto to public narratives via a 1951 article by Čučkov, the first director of Tanec, in which he

> promoted the prototype of the ideal-typic Macedonian dance. In fact, having the Mijak *Teškoto* dance in mind, Čučkov, without even mentioning the dance in question, described an imaginary "glorious Macedonian dance." Mystifying the tempo rubato of the dance . . . Čučkov gives it epic proportions . . . and promoted it as a symbol of the struggles for the national liberation of the Macedonian people. Manoil Čučkov thus not only promoted, but also institutionalized the *Teškoto* as a prototype of a Macedonian dance. The *Teškoto* has been the undisputed "master" of the Macedonian folk dance scene for over sixty years.

Čučkov emphasized the slow beginning of the dance to signify the gravity of oppression, and the fast ending to signify victory (Wilson 2014). The website of the Ministry of Culture states:

> The Hard One (Teškoto) is considered to be one of the most beautiful and most difficult Macedonian folk dances. . . . In essence, it is devoted to the farewell moments of the Macedonians who were leaving their country to work abroad. . . . However, over time it developed in a hymn not only of the people who worked abroad, but also of sufferings that piled up in the Macedonian souls through the centuries of subjugation.[4]

The connection between Teškoto and historical struggle was further bolstered by Blaže Koneski's 1948 poem, titled "Teškoto." Koneski was a major figure in language standardization, and his poem is still taught

FIGURE 3

Tanec poster featuring Teškoto. Used with permission of the archives of Tanec.

in Macedonian elementary schools. The poem invokes national liberation against enslavement (implied to be Turkish) via dance.[5]

As Teškoto became a showpiece for Tanec, several dramatic elements were introduced. Like other Balkan ensembles striving to "modernize" their folklore, Tanec took as its model the USSR's Moiseyev Ensemble, which was a folk ballet (Višinski and Dunin 1995, 8). When Tanec competed in the 1950 Llangollen Festival in Wales, where it won first prize, Teškoto was no longer led by one dancer. Rather, leadership passed from one dancer to another in the fast section, adding a frenzied finale; in addition, all dancers started doing turns and deep knee bends. These changes were introduced in the 1930s by Lazaropolje dancers who had moved to Belgrade (263). The most dramatic element, and the pose that has become iconic, is the leader climbing on top of the drum, with one leg raised (figure 3). This pose was refined for the 1950 Llangollen Festival.[6]

Dunin notes that "the version of Teškoto performed . . . in 1950 . . . has been consistently performed for almost forty years"; no other dance performed by Tanec has remained so stable (Višinski and Dunin 1995, 263). Since 1948, Tanec has also been generously supported by the government; has consistently employed a large cadre of staff, performers, and musicians; has toured the world in over 4,500 concerts; and has received major national and city awards (Tatarchevska 2011, 85; see also http://www.tanec.com.mk).

Current Status with Regard to UNESCO: No Status

Macedonia failed twice to attain UNESCO Masterpiece status for Teškoto, and currently it is not on Macedonia's National Registry of Cultural Heritage, the internal representative list supervised by the Ministry of Culture. Macedonia legally ratified the Convention for the Safeguarding of the Intangible Cultural Heritage in 2006 and the Convention on the Protection and Promotion of the Diversity of Cultural Expressions in 2007. Since 2005 the Institute of Folklore and the Institute of Macedonian Language have been in charge of preparing ICH documents; before 2005 various organizations and folklore ensembles prepared applications. According to the Ministry of Culture, the stated goals of ICH work are preservation and tourism. Macedonia currently has sixty-eight ICH elements on its Registry, consisting of thirty-nine folk creations (such as harvest singing), nineteen dialects of Macedonian language, and ten dialects of minority languages (Tatarchevska 2010). In 2013, one of these elements, the Feast of the Holy Forty Martyrs in Štip, was inscribed on the UNESCO ICH Representative List, followed by Kopačka, a dance from the village of Dramče, Pijanec, in 2014.

On-the-Ground Perspectives: ICH Status Failures

The first Macedonian attempt to engage with UNESCO occurred in 2002 when it applied for Masterpiece status for the wedding ritual in the village of Galičnik.[7] Teškoto was a central element of the application. UNESCO approved 15,000 US dollars for the preparation of the application by the Macedonian Folklore Ensembles Association (SOFAM). Although the entire wedding is too complicated to describe here, up until the 1940s the families of returning migrant workers frequently held weddings culminating on Petrovden (Saint Peter's Day), July 12. Up to fifty weddings took place simultaneously.

Galičnik was historically the largest and most prosperous of the twenty-four Mijak villages. Weddings there were up to eight days long, with elaborate rituals to ensure fertility and prosperity, heavily embroidered handwoven costumes, elaborate gift-giving, feasting, story-telling, and traditional vocal and instrumental music and dance, including Teškoto. Galičnik wedding customs precisely fit UNESCO's definition of ICH (Kličkova and Georgieva [1951] 1996).[8] However, the actual inhabitants of Galičnik, the grassroots connection, were missing.

In the late nineteenth century Galičnik had three thousand inhabitants, but during the twentieth century the population declined due to urbanization and migration. After World War II and the socialization of private land, the village lost its economic base; the last wedding was held in 1953, and by the 1960s only a few elderly residents remained. Today some descendants return to family homes during the summer. In 1963, a few former residents set about reviving the wedding ritual as a staged re-creation for Macedonian as well as foreign tourists. A five-hundred-seat stone amphitheater was constructed, and amateur ensembles became involved in the performance. The Galičnik Wedding has become an annual event held on the weekend closest to July 12; it is enacted in a two-day condensed version by members of the Skopje-based Kočo Racin dance ensemble plus several former villagers who formed an association. Currently thousands of people attend, and competitive applications are taken from couples with heritage from Galičnik who want to be married during the ritual. The event is covered by the media and heavily promoted by the Ministry of Tourism. Political speeches, a song contest, and anniversary celebrations have been added.

The 2002 UNESCO application was submitted by the Union of Macedonian Folklore Ensembles, whose stated aim was "to preserve, protect, support and present Macedonian folklore which reflects . . . the heritage and traditions of the Macedonian people and the nationalities who live in the Republic of Macedonia." The submitted list of "custodians of the know how," was dominated by ensemble leaders and folklorists, not villagers (UNESCO 2001, 13). The application consisted of florid language lauding the Galičnik wedding as "a masterpiece of human creative genius" embodying authentic folklore and national heritage. Teškoto was labeled "the Dance of Defiance"; the Ministry described Teškoto as "a symbol of the insubordination of Macedonians" (this refers to the defeat of Ottoman Turks). Referencing the organic tropes of romantic nationalism, the application stated that the wedding embodies the soul of the nation that finds expression in rural folklore. All this is quite paradoxical considering that the wedding is a re-creation.

How far the wedding has changed from its "natural" context and whether that disqualifies it from UNESCO's definition of ICH is part of a wider conversation about authenticity and purity. I agree with folklorists who claim that change signals a healthy folklore environment; however, not all changes are equivalent. Catherine Grant (2012, 38) writes that "Music tourism and 'festivalisation' are examples of how ideological acceptance of change in a tradition might manifest within the context of initiatives to strengthen a genre's vitality, and scholars now acknowledge that these phenomena deserve consideration well beyond any dogmatic dismissal that they (re)present a less 'authentic' tradition, and therefore one of lesser value." The Galičnik wedding, however, has not merely been "festivalized" for tourists—its locals are merely part-time residents.

Another issue to consider is ethnicity: although Galičnik is an Eastern Orthodox Slavic-speaking Macedonian village, all the musicians who provided music for the weeklong ritual were Muslim Roma from the nearby city of Debar.[9] These professional performers, traditionally from the Majovci clan, intimately knew the native dance repertoire and signaled every important ritual moment with appropriate melodies. There is even an adage that says "no wedding will take place in Galičnik unless the Majovci family plays." Thus Roma were not only integrated into the Galičnik wedding, but the villagers were dependent upon them for the oldest layer of their ritual, dance, and processional music. Despite these facts, however, the UNESCO application hardly mentioned Roma and nowhere mentioned them in relation to the goals of affirming cultural identity and preserving traditions. Roma were merely described in a few sentences as musicians.[10]

Heritage is assumed to be coterminous with bounded territorial groups—so-called folk communities (Noyes 2006)—and Roma have usually been excluded from the category *folk* (Silverman 2012, 2014). On the one hand, only nation-states can submit UNESCO applications; thus UNESCO empowers states, and states respond with "heritage strategies."[11] Moreover, the "masterpieces of humanity" designation and even the newer post-2008 "representative list designation" elide into the "nation," which must choose some aspects of its culture as "masterpieces" or "representative" and reject other aspects. Needless to say, minority culture can be problematic here. On the other hand, UNESCO specifically advocates for the "preservation of cultural diversity" and the "tolerance and harmonious interaction between cultures" (UNESCO 2001), so one might expect cultural communication between ethnic groups to have surfaced in the application, but this was not the case. The great potential for recognizing and promoting cultural exchange between Roma and Macedonians was ignored.

Similarly, Roma were omitted from the section on training the next generation in folk practices. In fact, the zurla and tapan players at re-created Galičnik weddings for the most part have not been from the local Majovci clan but rather have been Roma from the capital city of Skopje who are employed by dance ensembles. They play in a different style and do not know the full regional repertoire. However, in 2011 and 2014 the Majovci performed (Dave Wilson, pers. comm.). As the Majovci negotiate precarious professional performance opportunities, they need support in training the next generation, which ICH recognition could aid. The Majovci are still respected musicians in the region, are still training their sons, and are still hired for some local celebrations, despite the challenge of a decreasing number of patrons; in 2005 a compact disc of their music was released by the Mister Company, with the dual-language title *Zurli I Tapani na Galička Svadba, Majovci / Wedding in Galičnik, Macedonian Wedding Music with Pipes and Drums*. Ironically, while the living traditions of Roma (zurla and tapan performance) are in danger of being excluded or minimized, in the 2002 UNESCO application, the folklore of the majority Macedonians was coded as authentic, even though it was staged.

After the 2002 application was rejected by UNESCO, a second application for Masterpiece status was submitted in 2004. It specifically focused on Teškoto and was prepared by Tanec. According to Tatarchevska, it was written "not with a scientific approach but instead in a populist manner, full of emotions by the former dancers."[12] The application focused on nationalist sentiment and described the staged version of the dance that had become iconic, not the traditional dance. No folklorists were involved in the preparation. This application was also rejected by UNESCO. After these rejections, many cultural workers realized that ICH documents should be written by folklorists, and soon after Macedonia's ICH policy shifted to the Institute of Folklore and the Ministry of Culture. In 2008, UNESCO replaced the Masterpiece process with the Representative List in order to be more inclusive. However, Teškoto is not on Macedonia's Registry and there are no plans for including it.

I suggest that past applications for Teškoto (and inclusion on the Registry) could have possibly been successful if the wider dynamic, living, grassroots, and multiethnic framework of the dance had been considered. Teškoto is not an isolated dance but is part of a genre of dances called *Teški Ora* (difficult or heavy dances) found all over Macedonia, as opposed to *Lesni Ora* (easy or light dances). This category would have been too broad for UNESCO ICH status because it includes hundreds of dances. However, if we examine the structure of the specific Teškoto of western Macedonian Mijaks, we see that it is closely related to some dances of the minority ethnic group known as Torbeši (Muslim Mijaks). In fact, according to Tatarchevska, the very same traditional Teškoto continued to be danced until recently among Torbeši who still lived in western Macedonian villages.[13] However, because Torbeši live in villages that are less well known than Galičnik and Lazaropolje and because they are a Muslim minority, government officials paid no attention to them. This group could have been the missing "grassroots" component required for a successful UNESCO application. Tatarchevska also pointed out that as these Torbeši began to be exposed to the iconic version of Teškoto as performed by Tanec, they too adopted the standard form, "the Tanec recipe." It seems to me that the potential of recognizing and preserving the dance in its Mijak village context has been lost.

On the other hand, if one grants that this specific Teškoto is part of a subgenre marked by a slow nonmetric section followed by a fast metered section, one can still find these types of dances performed by Albanians and Torbeši in Skopje.[14] However, again, the fact that performers are Muslims problematizes national attention to their dance repertoire. In addition, this dance structure is not unique to Macedonia; it is also found in the province of northern Greece called Macedonia and in Kosovo and Albania. Thus it would be hard for FYROM to claim this dance form as uniquely its own. Many UNESCO elements have faced similar problems of cross-border claims; in response, there are several multi-Balkan nation applications in preparation. In sum, there is little chance now for Teškoto to appear on any representative list. It now has a vibrant existence in Macedonia as a staged dance, but in ethnic Macedonian village contexts it has died out.

Discussion: Tourism, Branding, and Ethnic Politics

All these UNESCO initiatives need to be understood in the context of the current postsocialist economic crisis, in which the possibility of increased tourism to Macedonia is seen as urgent. Tourism is heavily

FIGURE 4
Statue of Teškoto in Skopje. Photograph by author.

promoted by the Ministry of Culture, and folklore has become a good advertisement for the new country. Folk dance and music are crucial to tourism, and Teškoto is a central icon. "Today *Teškoto* is found in practically all tourist guidebooks, encyclopedias from former Yugoslavia, in all campaigns for cultural and village tourism, or for any kind of promotion of the country" (Tatarchevska 2011, 84). In fact, a statue of the iconic Teškoto pose of the lead dancer standing on the drum is found in downtown Skopje (figure 4). Since independence, the tourism industry has embraced branding and, in the process, has recruited the tropes of Macedonian nation building, celebrating the Byzantine past, and preserving present-day rural folklore; here music, dance, and imagery play pivotal roles.

For example, a series of alluring television advertisements has been broadcast recently on European channels. Titled Macedonia Timeless and commissioned by the Ministry of Culture and the state tourist agency, the advertisements brand the nation's culture as simultaneously ancient and modern through imagery and music. One, directed by noted filmmaker Milčo Mančevski, hints at Macedonian folk music through snippets of 7/8 melodies, the strumming of strings, images of a men's line dance with a tapan player, and a zurla player who pops up in a children's book.[15] But the music is mostly Western symphonic with the suggested beat of a tapan. Even though zurla and tapan are traditional Romani instruments, there are no Roma in this clip; the tapan player is blond. Additionally, neither Albanians nor other minorities nor any Muslim images appear in this advertisement. In fact, the zurla appears for only a few seconds in an image of a Western ensemble with a cello and Western timpani. Most of the imagery in the clip depicts ancient and Eastern Orthodox themes, upholding Macedonia's claim to antiquity.

A second Macedonia Timeless clip begins with a Galičnik wedding.[16] The video opens with a ritual scene from the wedding that has become iconic: the bride looking through a ring. The traditional ritual is that the groom goes to the door of the bride's home, and she looks through a ring and says, "I see you through this ring, so that I may enter into your heart." In the clip, there is a brief shot of zurla and tapan players, and we hear zurla music in 9/8. However, again, no Roma are pictured. In both these videos, folklore and folk music serve as a bridge between the ancient and the modern, but both present a monoethnic Macedonia in which elements of ethnic and religious minorities are minimized.

Currently, neither internal nor UNESCO ICH designations are really "needed" to brand Teškoto as a national treasure; it is already branded, and it serves as an emotional symbol for Macedonians (Wilson 2014). On the other hand, other forms of local folklore do need ICH designation because they are deemed "old-fashioned" or "endangered" or regionally iconic. For example, Kopačka (the digging dance), a striking and difficult line dance from eastern Macedonia that emphasizes small, fast, and sharp steps, is well known in its region and is performed by Tanec. But in 2012 I was surprised to hear villagers from Dramče announce that it was "certified" by UNESCO. They wanted to convince the audience that if UNESCO valued Kopačka, then we all should. They were clearly proud; they are striving to preserve the dance among young people and to expand performance possibilities. Both endeavors have been partially successful. Indeed, Kopačka was inscribed on Macedonia's Registry in December 2013 and UNESCO's Representative List in 2014.[17]

Dramče villagers employ the discourse of UNESCO in part because they have been trained to present Kopačka to outsiders by ICH workers both from their village association and from the Ministry of Culture; they have also learned to objectify and label their dance and to verbally express pride in their heritage. Most Macedonians, on the other hand, are ignorant about ICH initiatives, although they realize that folklore can stimulate tourism. Roma are perhaps even more ignorant about ICH, due to their marginalization. They are more interested in securing paid work and in avoiding prejudice than in achieving ICH status. Due to centuries of discrimination, Roma tend to be practical, and they realize that although they were indispensable as musicians for unstaged celebrations, they have been ignored in national branding endeavors. In addition, Roma are starting to be replaced in their traditional musical professional roles. In the future, as ICH initiatives become more widespread, Roma might be more savvy about claiming their rightful place in Macedonian folklore.

Comparing the 2002 Galičnik wedding application and the 2012 Kopačka application, I note that the latter shies away from romanticism and explains the dance in its living dynamic context. Unlike in Galičnik, in Dramče villagers of all ages and both sexes are involved on a grassroots level in preservation activities, and the dance is part of living village heritage. However, in both applications the role of Roma is minimized. As in Galičnik, in Dramče, Romani tapan players provide the traditional music for Kopačka (it is danced solely to several tapans, and the Semka clan are the most famous Romani drummers). The application states: "There is cooperation between Macedonians and Roma in the region specially in the performance of the dance. . . . Inscription can strengthen the intercultural connection between the musicians (predominantly ethnic Roma) and the dancers of Macedonian nationality" (UNESCO 2012). However, no ethnographic information about Roma is provided in the ten-page document. Similarly, in booklets produced by the Kopačka association in Dramče, neither the text nor the photographs highlight Roma. Thus, exclusions regarding Roma persist; however, grassroots activism around Kopačka contrasts with the lack of a living village Teškoto tradition. It is not surprising then, that Teškoto's fate has been totally different from Kopačka's.

Kopačka remains a dance known mostly in its region, despite its UNESCO designation. In contrast, Teškoto has emerged as a national treasure despite UNESCO application failures due to its branding as a traditional and iconic men's dance. Macedonians instantly claim Teškoto as theirs, and it lives on in images and stage performances. It also appears as a "pose" in a dramatic moment in urban Macedonian weddings. In urban weddings in the capital Skopje, folk musicians are often hired for a short show while the regular wedding band (that plays urban folk and popular music on synthesized instruments) takes a break. These folk musicians play acoustic instruments such as zurla and tapan, and at an emotional moment they encourage the groom (or another honored male guest) to climb up on the tapan in the "Teškoto pose." Teškoto has thus become a living symbol of Macedonian village folklore, defiance, and male bonding that is enacted by urban middle-class Macedonians to remind them of their roots; it might even become an urban ritual. The hired musicians for these weddings are not Roma but ethnic Macedonian ensemble musicians. The dance is impossible without zurla and tapan, but Roma are easily replaceable.

Cultural heritage projects are active sites for reinscribing and revising narratives about Macedonia's past, present, and future. Through its connection with traditional village life, ritual, male strength, and nationalist resistance, Teškoto has been elevated to an icon. However, its grassroots connection has been compromised in part because of the role of Tanec in the process of standardization. Ironically, icons require standardization for easy recognition and branding, but this works against the dynamism of living folklore. Two UNESCO applications failed due to their focus on staged folklore, but the potential for viewing Teškoto as ICH might have been realized if ethnic politics permitted it. Today, Teškoto is more a national symbol than a village reality.

Acknowledgments

The author would like to thank Macedonian dance ethnologist Ivona Opetcheska Tatarchevska for sharing her vast knowledge and insights; Jane Sugarman also provided valuable feedback. The interpretations and opinions expressed are solely the author's. Research was done on numerous trips to Macedonia between 1971 and 2012 (some trips were supported by the University of Oregon and the Guggenheim Foundation) and via Internet resources. Several paragraphs were reworked from Silverman 2012 with permission of the publisher.

Notes

1. See the website for Macedonia's state statistical office at http://www.stat.gov.mk/OblastOpsto_en.aspx?id=31.

2. Roma face extreme discrimination in housing, employment, schooling, health care, and other public services (Silverman 2012).

3. A film from 1948 titled *Jugoslovenski Narodni Plesovi* shows Žikoski leading Teškoto before it became standardized. Another of the dancers in the film is Dojčin Matevski, also from Lazaropolje, who led Teškoto in Tanec for several decades.

4. See http://www.soros.org.mk/konkurs/076/angver/Teskoto.html.

5. The poem begins:

O Teškoto! As soon as the zurli start playing wildly
As soon as the tapani thunder with an underground echo
Why is a hot sadness burning in my chest
Why is a river pouring into my eyes
Why do I feel like crying like a child
Bending my hands and covering my face
Biting my lips and squeezing my cursed heart
Not to shout.

6. Dunin further elaborates that in Mijak village contexts the drum was too large and thin to bear the weight of a dancer, but in Skopje drums are smaller and thicker. The pose was based on "the recollection . . . that the leader had complete control of the dance and the accompanying musicians. . . . The leader could climb on top of the musicians as they played for him in a bent down position" (Višinski and Dunin 1995, 263). This indicates the embodied subordinate "client" relationship of Roma to their patrons.

7. I would like to thank Mark Levy, who was a reviewer of the 2002 Macedonian UNESCO application, for sharing it with me along with his insights and evaluations.

8. For a 1955 documentary film on the Galičnik wedding, see *Galicka Svadba* (Galičnik wedding), directed by Aco Petrovski. Another documentary was made in 2009, titled *Galicka Svadba 2009*. These films were sponsored and funded by the Macedonian government.

9. These Roma are Albanian-speaking and refer to themselves as *Egjupci* (Egyptians). Historically they were Roma who moved up the social scale by adopting the Albanian language and distancing themselves from the stigmatized Roma label.

10. The descriptive part of the application is based on Vera Kličkova's 1951 study, which minimizes the role of Roma.

11. William Logan (2007, 48) states that "national interests continue to loom large in human rights, cultural rights, and cultural heritage issues. . . . National governments place enormous importance on UNESCO listings. . . . Their interest is multi-faceted and includes the economic benefits of tourism but particularly the international status." The "heritage strategies" employed by various states are explored in a recent volume (Bendix, Eggert, and Peselmann 2012).

12. Interview with the author, April 10, 2012.

13. Interview with the author, April 10, 2012.

14. Ethnomusicologist Jane Sugarman and historian Eran Fraenkel filmed these types of dances done by Albanian men in Skopje between 1980 and 1982. In a recent personal communication, Sugarman stated that she located YouTube videos of this community still doing these dances; see http://www.youtube.com/watch?v=uEm6p6tg85k and http://www.youtube.com/watch?v=99IukX0ZNmQ. Some community members moved to Turkey in the 1950s and 1960s and still perform these dances in Turkey. See http://www.youtube.com/watch?v=KJHyJENN8Sc and http://www.youtube.com/watch?v=UqnKlHrsRwk.

15. See http://www.youtube.com/watch?v=PtYrDVqr7IQ.

16. See http://macedonia-timeless.com/videos.

17. See http://www.unesco.org/culture/ich/RL/00995.

References Cited

Bendix, Regina F., Aditya Eggert, and Arnika Peselmann, eds. 2012. *Heritage Regimes and the State*. Göttingen: Universitätsverlag Göttingen.

Brown, Keith. 2003. *The Past in Question: Modern Macedonia and the Uncertainties of Nation*. Princeton, NJ: Princeton University Press.

Grant, Catherine. 2012. "Rethinking Safeguarding: Objections and Responses to Protecting and Promoting Endangered Musical Heritage." *Ethnomusicology Forum* 21 (1): 31–51.

Hofman, Ana. 2008. "Music of 'Working People': Musical Folklore and the Creation of Yugoslav Identity." In *Musical Folklore as a Vehicle?*, edited by Mirjana Veselinović-Hofman, 59–67. Belgrade: Serbian Musicological Society.

Hupchick, Dennis P. 1994. "Nation or Millet? Contrasting Western European and Islamic Political Cultures in the Balkans." In *Culture and History in Eastern Europe*, 121–55. New York: St. Martin's Press.

Janković, Ljubica, and Danica Janković. 1934. *Narodne Igre* [Folk dances] 1. Belgrade: Stamparija Drag.

Kličkova, Vera, and Milica Georgieva. (1951) 1996. *Wedding Customs in Galičnik*. Skopje: NIP.

Logan, William. 2007. "Closing Pandora's Box: Human Rights Conundrums in Cultural Heritage Protection." In *Cultural Heritage and Human Rights*, edited by Helene Silverman and D. F. Ruggles, 33–52. New York: Springer.

Neofotistos, Vasiliki. 2012. *The Risk of War: Everyday Sociality in the Republic of Macedonia*. Philadelphia: University of Pennsylvania Press.

Noyes, Dorothy. 2006. "The Judgment of Solomon: Global Protection for Tradition and the Problem of Community Ownership." *Cultural Analysis* 5:27–56.

Seeman, Sonia. 2012. "Macedonian *Čalgija*: A Musical Refashioning of National Identity." *Ethnomusicology Forum* 21 (3): 295–326.

Silverman, Carol. 2012. *Romani Routes: Cultural Politics and Balkan Music in Diaspora*. New York: Oxford University Press.

———. 2014. "Balkan Romani Culture, Human Rights, and the State: Whose Heritage?" In *Cultural Heritage in Transit: Intangible Rights as Human Rights*, edited by Deborah Kapchan, 125–47. Philadelphia: University of Pennsylvania Press.

Tatarchevska, Ivona Opetcheska. 2010. "General Policies Regarding the Intellectual Property Rights of the Traditional Knowledge and Traditional Cultural Expressions (Intangible Cultural Heritage) in Republic of Macedonia." Paper presented at WIPO Inter-Regional Experts Meeting, July 8–9, in Warsaw, Poland.

———. 2011. "The Idea behind Our Folk Dances: Public Narratives about Folk Dances in Macedonia." In *Proceedings, Second Symposium of the International Council for Traditional Music, Study Group on Music and Dance in Southeastern Europe*, edited by Liz Mellish, Velika Serafimova, and Mehmet Öcal Özbilgin, 78–85. İzmir: Ege University.

UNESCO. 2001. *Proclamation of Masterpieces of the Oral and Intangible Heritage of Humanity: Guide for the Presentation of Candidature Files*. Paris: UNESCO. http://unesdoc.unesco.org/images/0012/001246/124628eo.pdf.

———. 2012. "Nomination File No. 00736 for Inscription on the Representative List of the Intangible Cultural Heritage of Humanity in 2012." Convention for the Safeguarding of the Intangible Cultural Heritage Intergovernmental Committee for the Safeguarding of the Intangible Cultural Heritage. Seventh session, Paris. Paris: UNESCO. http://www.unesco.org/culture/ich/doc /download.php?versionID=16775.

Višinski, Stanimir, and Elsie Dunin. 1995. *Dances in Macedonia: Performance, Genre, Tanec.* Prilep: 11 Oktomvri.

Wilson, Dave. 2014. "Teškoto and National Sentiment in Macedonia: Ascribing Meaning, Experiencing Tradition." In *Third Symposium of the International Council for Traditional Music (ICTM) Study Group on Music and Dance in Southeastern Europe,* edited by Elise Dunin, Liz Mellish, and Ivona Opetcheska-Tatarchevska, 242–49. Skopje: Kontura.

CAROL SILVERMAN, Professor of Cultural Anthropology and Folklore, has done research for over twenty-five years in the Balkans and with Balkan Roma in several diasporic sites. She explores politics, music, human rights, gender, and state policy with a focus on representation. Her 2012 book *Romani Routes: Cultural Politics and Balkan Music in Diaspora* won the Merriam Prize from the Society for Ethnomusicology.

6 Shifting Actors and Power Relations: Contentious Local Responses to the Safeguarding of Intangible Cultural Heritage in Contemporary China

THIS ESSAY ADDRESSES the contentious local responses to intangible cultural heritage (ICH) protection in a local context. The following ethnographic case study concerns the living tradition of worshipping the ancient sage-kings Yao and Shun in several villages in Hongtong County, Shanxi Province, China. Named as an item of national ICH in 2008, the official title of this local tradition is Hongtong Zouqin Xisu, "the custom of visiting sacred relatives in Hongtong." I explore the ways local people have responded to the safeguarding of ICH, with a focus on shifting actors and power relations within interconnected communities.

Location: Hongtong County, Shanxi Province, China

Hongtong is a county in the prefecture-level city of Linfen, in the southwestern part of Shanxi Province, located in the northern part of China (figure 1).[1] Hongtong is the most populated county in the city of Linfen. It occupies an area of 1,563 square kilometers, and in 2010 its population was 733,421 people.[2] It has nine *zhen* (towns) and seven *xiang* (townships), including 463 *cunmin weiyuanhui* (villagers' committees) that govern 902 *zirancun* (natural villages) (Zhang et al. 2005, 19–30). Hongtong is well known for the status it held as an immigration transfer center during the Hongwu (1368–98) and Yongle (1403–24) periods of the Ming dynasty, when the state organized mass migrations to other provinces to offset population loss due to continuous warfare. These forced migrations were a traumatic event for many people at that time, who remembered the homelands they were forced to abandon and passed this information to their descendants. Today, a popular folk song sung throughout China contains the lines, "Where is my old hometown? The big pagoda tree in Hongtong,

113

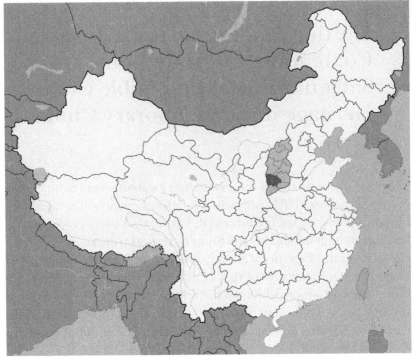

FIGURE 1
Location of Linfen in Shanxi, People's Republic of China. Public domain image.
http://en.wikipedia.org/wiki/File:China_Shanxi_Linfen.svg.

Shanxi. What is the name of my ancestral place? The stork nest under
the pagoda tree" (Zhang and Lin 1988, 1).[3] The pagoda tree and the
stork nest in Hongtong became important symbols of "roots" for many
Chinese descendants from Hongtong living all over the world.

ICH Element: Hongtong Zouqin Xisu

Hongtong Zouqin Xisu, "the custom of visiting sacred relatives in
Hongtong," was listed in the national ICH list released by the State
Council of China on June 7, 2008. The original full title of the tradition was *"Jie gugu ying niangniang" zouqin huodong*, which literally
means "receiving 'aunties' and welcoming 'grandmas,' visiting relatives
activity." "Aunties" and "grandmas" refer to Ehuang and Nüying, the
two daughters of the prehistoric sage-king Yao, who were married off

FIGURE 2
The statues of Ehuang and Nüying at their temple in Yangxie, Hongtong, Shanxi, May 27, 2013. Photograph by author.

by Yao to his successor Shun more than four thousand years ago (see figure 2).

Yao and Shun are believed to have lived about 4,700 years ago, and their time has been established as the starting period of Chinese cultural history (Sima Qian 1959, 15–43). According to local oral tradition, Yangxie (pronounced as Yanghai), was formerly known as Zhoufu Village. Long ago, a goat gave birth to a kid with only one horn, whose name was *xie* (pronounced as *hai*). The horn of this sacred goat was said to have the power to distinguish between good and evil. After hearing the news, King Yao and his wife came to the village. When they arrived at the place where the unicorn had been born, King Yao's wife, who was pregnant, gave birth to a daughter. The baby was brilliantly beautiful, and she could speak after only three days and was able to walk several days later. On seeing these magic events, King Yao was extremely surprised; deeming the village to be a sacred place, he renamed it Yangxie, which literally means "goat-unicorn" in Chinese, and he called his newborn daughter Nüying, or "Maiden Bloom." Then the whole family came to live in Yangxie.

When King Yao became old, he saw that his own sons were unworthy of being emperor, so he asked his ministers to propose a suitable successor. That is when he heard of Shun's feats.[4] But King Yao did not simply want to believe the tales about Shun, so he decided to test him. He gave a district to Shun to govern and married his two daughters Ehuang and Nüying to him. Yao believed that if Shun could govern the household well, he also should be able to govern the kingdom. In the end, King Yao was very impressed by all of Shun's achievements, and he chose Shun to be his successor. After Shun died on his expedition to the south, Ehuang and Nüying drowned themselves in the Xiang River and became goddesses.

Every year on the third day of the third lunar month, known as *San Yue San*, villagers in Yangxie, where the Temple of King Yao was located, carry Ehuang and Nüying's *jialou*, or "storied palanquin," to Lishan, where King Shun's temple was located, to receive their two "aunties" and bring them back to visit the home of their parents in Yangxie. A large temple fair is held in Lishan on the third day of the third lunar month. On the twenty-eighth day of the fourth lunar month, which is believed to be King Yao's birthday, a temple fair is held in the Temple of Yao in Yangxie. Villagers from Lishan escort their two "grandmas" back home to Lishan.

Marked by the boundary of the Fen River, people on the east side of the river call Ehuang and Nüying "aunties" as if they were the offspring of King Yao; people on the west side refer to Ehuang and Nüying as "grandmas" as if they were the offspring of King Shun. In particular, Yangxie residents call Ehuang and Nüying "aunties," while people from Lishan, Wan'an, Xiqiaozhuang, and most other villages call them "grandmas." In this way, the Fen River functions not only as a geographical marker but also as a cultural marker that differentiates generational statuses in the "sacred" family. This differentiation was explained to me by the influential local figure Li Xuezhi in Lishan in my first interview with him on April 18 (the second day of the third lunar month), 2007. Because of the prehistoric royal marriage, Yangxie people and Lishan people call each other *qinqi* (relatives), and their relationships are interpreted as *shengqin* or *shenqin*, "sacred relatives." Li furthermore explained that people from Yangxie and Lishan were banned from marrying each other because it would be regarded as incest.

During each of these festivals, the procession usually passes through more than twenty villages, and in each one local residents burn incense, provide free tea and snacks to participants, kowtow toward Ehuang and Nüying's jialou, and ask for blessings. In large villages people also play drums and gongs, competing with the players from Yangxie or Lishan performing in the processions. In some villages free lunch and afternoon meals are provided for participants in the processions. The residents of Lishan and Wan'an also accommodate Yangxie people for one night on the third day of the third lunar month, and Yangxie participants host their Lishan and Wan'an "relatives" for one night during the celebrations of King Yao's birthday.

Local villagers explained to me that they have held these activities for more than four thousand years, even though the Shun Temple in Lishan was destroyed during the Second Sino-Japanese War (1937–45), the Yao Temple in Yangxie was dismantled during the War of Liberation (1947–49), and the local tradition was banned during the Cultural Revolution (1966–76) under Mao Zedong's rule. For many years, the Chinese Communist state had tried to eradicate cultural expressions of the old pre-Communist China, stigmatizing them as superstitious or "feudalistic," while it built a new, socialist culture (Chau 2006). Despite the harsh political conditions, however, the local celebrations continued without interruption. When the tradition was officially banned during the Cultural Revolution, several villagers from Yangxie practiced it secretly, and some were even sent to prison because of their continued participation. After Mao Zedong died in 1976, economic reforms began, accompanied by significant ideological relaxation. This local tradition was officially revived in the 1980s and 1990s. The current Yao Temple in Yangxie was rebuilt in 1989, the Shun Temple in Lishan was rebuilt in 1995, and the local temple fairs were revived in the 1990s.

In local tradition, *shè* 社 is the key folk group that sponsors local festivals and celebrations; it is created by devotees of a temple to connect people to serve the deities of the temple. As a "microgeographic unit," a shè could be identical to a natural village, or several small villages could combine to form a shè, or a single large village could include several groups of shè (Johnson 2009, 184). Each shè serves a particular god in a particular temple, and different shè sometimes rotate to serve the same god in the same temple. In the Lishan area, six villages combined to form three shè, and the large Wan'an village includes two shè. Yangxie village used to include one shè, but the old shè has been divided into the Southern shè and the Northern shè to align with the division of the natural village that took place in 1963. In addition, Xiqiaozhuang village has formed one shè since the Temple of Ehuang and Nüying was built there in 1936 (Yan 2012). In Lishan, Yangxie, and Wan'an, different shè alternate to run annual ritual processions and temple affairs every year. The temple reconstruction associations were formed in the 1990s and 2000s during the public revival of local tradition. Their main purpose is to oversee the reconstruction of local temples and the management of incense donation money collected in the temples. Currently, there are three temple reconstruction associations in the temples of Ehuang and Nüying in Hongtong. In Lishan, a temple reconstruction association was officially approved in 1992. In Wan'an one was formed in 2003. In Yangxie one was founded in 2005. These temple reconstruction associations are based on the organization of shè and function as the general shè, overseeing the organization of annual ritual processions, temple fairs, and other temple affairs in general.

Current Status with Regard to UNESCO: No Status

Hongtong Zouqin Xisu is not currently inscribed on the UNESCO Representative List. However, it was inscribed on the Provincial List of Intangible Cultural Heritage in Shanxi Province in 2006, and in 2008 it was included in the second list of items of China's Intangible Cultural Heritage. These lists themselves were inspired by UNESCO's 2003 ICH Convention. Although Hongtong Zouqin Xisu is not on the Representative List, its continued performance and current situation has been deeply influenced by the global Convention.

Hongtong Zouqin Xisu was studied by Chinese folklorist Chen Yongchao (2000) when he conducted his dissertation fieldwork in Hongtong in 2000. In 2006 Zhou Xibin, the Communist Party Secretary in Ganting Town, saw the term *intangible cultural heritage* on the ticket of *Naxi Guyue*, "Naxi Ancient Music," when he visited one of his friends during the Spring Festival.[5] After finding out more about ICH and the lists, he decided that the local tradition in Yangxie (a part of Ganting Town) deserved to be listed both on the national and UNESCO ICH lists. Therefore, he mobilized local people to apply for its inclusion on the national list, and Wang Chunliang, the Director of the Cultural Center in Hongtong County, became one of his core partners. In 2006, Zhou invited a variety of journalists and cultural celebrities to participate in the local tradition and reflect on it in essays collected and published in a volume he edited (Zhou 2006). With strong promotion by the local government, the local tradition was inscribed on the Provincial List of ICH in Shanxi Province in 2006.[6]

Application for ICH on the national level was a long process. Zhou Xibin managed to contact Liu Kuili, the former president of the Chinese Folklore Society, in addition to other folklorists, to help local people complete the application materials. Chen Yongchao, who by this time was a professor at Beijing University, volunteered to help, and he took his students (me among them) to record the tradition during local festivals and temple fairs in 2007. Collaborating with folklorists, the Hongtong Center for the Safeguarding of ICH, founded by the Hongtong Cultural Center in 2006, represented the local government in the submission of the ICH application to the Ministry of Culture, which oversees the safeguarding of ICH in China. The application was submitted on September 15, 2007 (Wang 2009).

Although the application was approved by the national evaluation committee, Hongtong Zouqin Xisu disappeared from the tentative list of national ICH in 2008. No one knew for sure what had happened, but according to rumor the application was rejected by a senior official in the Ministry of Culture who came from Shanxi and did not want to promote too many traditions from his home province. After receiving the bad news, Hongtong officials went to Beijing and collaborated with folklorists to argue vociferously for its inclusion on the basis that it is a long, nearly uninterrupted tradition. Finally, on June 7, 2008, Hongtong Zouqin Xisu was inscribed on the second national ICH name list.

At this point Zhou Xibin, the initiator of the whole project, was eager to further promote the local tradition by nominating it for UNESCO's ICH Representative List. However, he was soon appointed deputy head of Hongtong County, and he subsequently left his town-level position. This dream of Hongtong Zouqin Xisu being inscribed on the UNESCO list became the ultimate goal for a few local intellectuals in Yangxie who had actively participated in the ICH application; whenever outside scholars visit to conduct research there, they convey this dream to them in hopes of support. When I conducted my fieldwork in Yangxie in 2012 and 2013, two asked me to assist them to achieve this goal, but no one has yet put forth the effort and Hongtong Zouqin Xisu has yet to be nominated for the UNESCO list.

On-the-Ground Perspectives:
A New Element in Local Conflicts

During my fieldwork in Hongtong, I interviewed many local people. When asked if they knew what ICH (*feiwuzhi wenhua yichan* 非物质文化遗产 in Chinese) and UNESCO were, most could not answer my questions. Only a few local officials and intellectuals knew of ICH and they explained that this foreign term had entered local discourse in 2005 when people were mobilized to assist in the ICH application. Yan Zhenghong, who is a retired Communist Party secretary, a temple executor, and the archivist at the Old Temple of King Yao in Yangxie, interpreted ICH as "invisible history and legends" in distinction to "material objects." When describing Hongtong Zouqin Xisu, Yan emphasized that contemporary people practiced it in reality, not in imagination, because it had been handed down for many generations. Yan regarded the local ICH as the region's cultural treasure, which could stimulate local people to stay together "harmoniously." Wang Wenhua, an old shè head in Yangxie, regarded ICH as the local tradition handed down for more than four thousand years, and "long history" (*niantouduo*) became a key phrase in local interpretations of ICH.[7] However, for most ordinary people, ICH was a foreign term remote from their knowledge and discourse. They similarly had no knowledge of UNESCO and its relationship to ICH.

The discourse of ICH has intensified the preexisting gap between local officials and ordinary people in local contexts, and this gap is sometimes expressed ironically during public celebrations. In 2008, for example, Liu Kuili and Chen Yongchao led some graduate students to conduct follow-up fieldwork in Yangxie and sponsored a performance of local opera at the temple fair. The temple fair office invited the two folklorists to give a short talk on stage before the performance. Wang Chunliang, the director of the Hongtong Cultural Center and the director of the local ICH Protection Center, suddenly jumped on stage. He was quite drunk and began talking at great length. At one point, he said: "What is ICH? Do you know it? Not only do you not know what ICH is, but even your grandpa and grandma do not know." An elderly woman sitting in the audience responded: "Your grandma is sitting here." This woman was no relation to him, but she was expressing, with irony, the audience's dismissal of this cultural official's arrogant speech. For her, what ICH was did not matter; her concern was with the live performance of local opera. She wanted to stop the "silly" speech and proceed with the performance.

What I have concluded from my fieldwork is that knowledge of ICH and UNESCO is not significant in the daily lives of most ordinary people. Those who were mobilized to assist in the ICH application expected to receive a large amount of money from the central government to do whatever they wished within their local communities. However, many express that they have yet to receive any funds, even after the success of the ICH application on the national level. When I interviewed Wang Chunliang about the financial situation on August 2012, he explained that the Ministry of Culture sent money to the Culture Office at the provincial level, but this office could not figure out how to distribute the money it had received for a number of different ICH projects in the region. In the end, it decided to evenly distribute the high interest from the ICH funds (allocated by the state from 2009 to 2012) among all national ICH elements in Shanxi. Accordingly, approximately 430,000 yuan (about 70,000 US dollars) was assigned to the Hongtong Zouqin Xisu project in November 2012 and received by the Hongtong Center for the Safeguarding of ICH. This was problematic because the tradition is shared by different communities in Hongtong, and people from Yangxie, Lishan, and Wan'an have all played important roles in continuing the tradition. These communities are located in different towns, and none of them had enough power to establish the protection center, which was crucial for the ICH safeguarding project. Moreover, the ICH application had fueled local conflicts between the communities, and it was hard for them to reach any agreement. The Hongtong Center for the Safeguarding of ICH was thus authorized by the local government as the representative institution to protect Hongtong Zouqin Xisu. After receiving the money, however, the Center did not distribute it to local temple reconstruction associations for rebuilding temples, which was what most local people had hoped for; instead, Director Wang Chunliang planned to build a living museum for Hongtong Zouqin Xisu. Wang's decision has disappointed local people, who are still trying to get the money back for temple affairs. The issue has yet to be settled.

The local conflicts among Yangxie, Lishan, and Wan'an did not originate during the ICH application but they were exacerbated in the process. On the second day of the third lunar month, the villagers of Yangxie carry the "storied palanquin" of two "aunties" in a procession accompanied by traditional music of drums and gongs. As they make their way toward Lishan, they pass through several other villages. After arriving at Lishan, they stay for one night. On the next day, the third day of the third lunar month, after receiving the two "aunties" from their temple in Lishan, Yangxie villagers return home again passing through several villages and staying one night in Wan'an. Traditionally, the events are primarily held in Yangxie and Lishan, while Wan'an is just "a way station for resting horses and eating meals" (*xiema liangdian*). However, Wan'an residents believe that another temporary palace of Shun is located there because one of his wives used to live in Wan'an in order to take care of Shun's parents. Residents do not consider Wan'an as only a resting place for the procession, but think it should have at least the same status as Lishan in the local tradition.

Villagers from Yangxie and Lishan have their own interpretations of why Wan'an is a stopping place: according to them, a long time ago, due to natural disaster, villagers from Yangxie became very exhausted after welcoming their "aunties" from Lishan. They encountered a rich man in Wan'an who invited them to have dinner and stay in his house for the night. The next year he made a fortune, which he attributed to having been blessed by the two goddesses. As a result, more people from Wan'an began to participate in the local tradition. This explanation has been widely accepted in the area. Although residents of Wan'an have enough economic power to build a magnificent temple, they do not have enough political and cultural power to argue for their status. In 2007, when Yangxie and Lishan collaborated to apply for the national ICH listing, Wan'an was totally excluded.

This exclusion is one episode in a longstanding feud between villagers in Wan'an with villagers in Yangxie. Yan Zhenghong provided some history on this feud. In 1991 Yan led Yangxie temple executors, in coordination with temple executors from other places, to change the festival date from the twenty-eighth day of the fourth lunar month to ten days earlier. The participating villages then suffered an ice storm, which many local people interpreted as miraculous retribution from

It is ironic that the local tradition was "protected" and transmitted primarily by the newly established Hongtong Center for the Safeguarding of ICH instead of by members of the communities who have long practiced it. Of course, the conundrum here is that the Center has not historically contributed to the tradition, but it is now charged with safeguarding it; in contrast, the shè and temple reconstruction associations that have maintained the tradition have no voice in the safeguarding process. In 2006, the Center coordinated a research team to conduct fieldwork and collect data along the procession of local parades and finish the drafts of ICH application materials for the national list (Wang 2009). The Yangxie temple reconstruction association paid all costs and hosted the Center staff when they came to Yangxie during the following years. Moreover, the temple reconstruction association is a key folk institution that is pivotal in producing and reproducing temple fairs and festivals; its members are volunteers from local communities who are devoted to continuing local tradition. Different local state agents interacted with the temple reconstruction association during the ICH project, and the latter paid the bills in the process. However, the heritage-making process has not empowered this folk institution to protect local tradition with and for local people; it has instead disempowered temple reconstruction associations and put local communities at the bottom of the power relationship, exaggerating already existing inequalities. The ICH project thus became a means for the local ICH center to exploit the local population and harvest the profits from the state. The process of local disempowerment described above helped to shape some fundamental precepts of the "heritage regime" (Bendix, Eggert, and Peselmann 2012).

In the "Comparative Assessment" to the volume *Heritage Regimes and the State*, Chiara De Cesari (2012) points out the "ambiguous" and "conflicted" relationship between many local civil society organizations dedicated to heritage preservation and the local UNESCO or ICH office, which may be viewed as allied to local authorities. De Cesari states that UNESCO frequently ends up reinforcing the power and reach of the nation-state and its bureaucracy, which is contradictory to its own principle of involving local communities and "grassroots" in heritage making—particularly in the 2003 ICH Convention. Contrary to UNESCO's goal of establishing a common heritage for humanity, the process of heritage making frequently gives rise to numerous tensions and conflicts (De Cesari 2012). My research is critical because it is a study of local and regional and national conflicts regarding a "pre-UNESCO" stage of ICH discourse. The conflicts I am observing between the people on the ground are conflicts that are caused by UNESCO despite the fact that this ICH has not even been nominated for the UNESCO list. In other words, even though the ICH in question has not been nominated for the UNESCO list, the UNESCO Convention itself set off a chain of events and national lists that ultimately had a profound effect on the communities involved.

In the process of protecting ICH on the ground, the alliance between discourse, practice, and power has not come to an end but has reappeared in a new mask. My question is not simply about who owns tradition and heritage, or how it is conceived locally. From a practical dimension, I am interested in how tradition and heritage can be transmitted and promoted respectfully with the active participation of local communities. With regard to the question of respect, Michael F. Brown (2003, 10) suggests that we should not ask "who owns native culture?" but "how can we promote respectful treatment of native cultures and indigenous forms of self-expression" within our everyday lives? All of us, native and nonnative alike, have a stake in decisions about the control and transmission of tradition and heritage, for those decisions will determine the future health of our natural and cultural world.

Notes

1. Linfen is located in the southwestern part of Shanxi, on the lower reaches of the Fen River, bounded by Changzhi and Jincheng to the east, the Yellow River to the west, Jinzhong and Lüliang to the north, and Yuncheng to the south.

2. These numbers are drawn from the Sixth National Population Census of the People's Republic of China, conducted by the National Bureau of Statistics of China (http://old.lfxww.com/xinwen/bsxw/2011/7/88584.shtml).

3. *Wen wo laojia zai he chu, shanxi hongtong da huaishu. Zuxian guju jiao shenme, dahuai shu xia laoguanwo.*

4. Shun was a legendary leader of ancient China, regarded by Sima Qian, a Chinese historian of the Han dynasty (206 BCE–220 CE), as one of the Five Emperors. Yao and Shun's stories were canonized by Sima Qian in the first chapter of his *Shiji*. Both Yao and Shun have been represented in Chinese history as morally perfect sage-kings. Yao's benevolence and diligence and Shun's filial piety and modesty were highly extolled by Confucian philosophers in later centuries and served as a model for Chinese kings and emperors.

5. *Naxi guyue* is the traditional music of the Naxi ethnic group in southwestern China. It is a kind of ritual music intertwined with local religions, and has been represented as a "living fossil" of traditional Chinese music (Rees 2000, 4–5).

6. I interviewed Zhou Xibin on August 5, 2012, concerning the detailed process of the ICH application.

7. I interviewed Wang Wenhua on April 16, 2013, and Yan Zhenghong on April 20, 2013.

8. The total costs for ICH application are unknown. From 2006 to 2008, the local government invested a lot of money to host cultural celebrities, scholars, journalists, and other visitors coming to experience the local tradition in Hongtong. The ICH application centered on Yangxie, and the temple association in Yangxie paid almost all the costs for research, application materials, and accommodation fees.

References Cited

Bendix, Regina F., Aditya Eggert, and Arnika Peselmann, eds. 2012. *Heritage Regimes and the State*. Göttingen: Universitätsverlag Göttingen.

Brown, Michael F. 2003. *Who Owns Native Culture?* Cambridge, MA: Harvard University Press.

Chau, Adam Yuet. 2006. *Miraculous Response: Doing Popular Religion in Contemporary China*. Stanford, CA: Stanford University Press.

Chen Yongchao. 2000. *Yao Shun chuan shuo yan jiu* [A study on the legends of Yao and Shun]. Nanjing: Nanjing Normal University Press.

De Cesari, Chiara. 2012. "Thinking through Heritage Regimes." In *Heritage Regimes and the State*, edited by Regina F. Bendix, Aditya Eggert, and Arnika Peselmann, 399–413. Göttingen: Universitätsverlag Göttingen.

Hauser-Schäublin, Brigitta, ed. 2012. *World Heritage Angkor and Beyond: Circumstances and Implications of UNESCO Listings in Cambodia*. Göttingen: Göttingen University Press.

Johnson, David G. 2009. *Spectacle and Sacrifice: The Ritual Foundations of Village Life in North China*. Cambridge, MA: Harvard University Asia Center.

Rees, Helen. 2000. *Echoes of History: Naxi Music in Modern China*. New York: Oxford University Press.

Sima Qian. 1959. *Shiji 1* [The records of the grand historian vol. 1]. Beijing: Zhong hua shu ju.

Wang Chunliang. 2009. "Hongtong sanyuesan zouqin xisu shenyi shimo" [How the custom of visiting sacred relatives in Hongtong became an element of intangible cultural heritage]. In *Shun geng Lishan zai Hongtong*, edited by Li Xuezhi, 325–32. Taiyuan: Sanjin chu ban she.

Yan Zhenghong, ed. 2012. *Huang Ying yishi* [Anecdotes of Ehuang and Nüying]. Booklet.

Zhang Qing and Lin Zhongyuan, eds. 1988. *Hongtong gu da huai shu zhi* [Annals of Ancient Big Pagoda Tree in Hongtong]. Taiyuan: Shanxi ren min chu ban she.

Zhang Qing, Wang Gensheng, et al., eds. 2005. *Hongtong xianzhi* [Hongtong County annals]. Taiyuan: Shanxi chun qiu dian zi yin xiang chu ban she.

Zhou Xibin, ed. 2006. *Yao Shun zhi feng jin you cun* [The customs of Yao and Shun through current times]. Beijing: Zhongguo xiju chubanshe.

ZIYING YOU is Visiting Assistant Professor of Chinese Studies at the College of Wooster, a position that is supported by the Andrew W. Mellon Foundation Postdoctoral Fellowship Program in Languages. She received her PhD from the Department of East Asian Languages and Literatures at The Ohio State University in spring 2015. She has broad research interests in the intellectual history of Chinese folklore studies, individual creativity in storytelling and performing arts, the dynamics of folk beliefs and popular religion, foodways, folkloric documentary, and grassroots agency in the safeguarding of intangible cultural heritage.

Critical Discussion

7 Understanding UNESCO: A Complex Organization with Many Parts and Many Actors

ONE OF THE great difficulties in evaluating the effectiveness of UNESCO intangible cultural heritage (ICH) programs at the local level is that the acronym (or "brand," as Michael Dylan Foster suggests in his essay) *UNESCO* is widely used, but the particular actors to which the term is applied are rarely indicated. UNESCO is not monolithic, and it has a number of distinct components that range from centralized to extremely decentralized. The final text of the 2003 Convention on the Safeguarding of Intangible Cultural Heritage (hereafter just 2003 Convention), was hammered out during months of debate and reflects a complex consensus. Its "Representative Lists" are described in the abstract wording of the 2003 Convention. But the methods used to select nominations and the actions taken to "safeguard" them are decided at different levels (national, provincial, or local) in different countries, each with its own history, government, and cultural policies. My contribution to this volume is an attempt to describe the various components of UNESCO and to illustrate some of its actions by referring to the essays in this collection. I will suggest that ethnographic discussions of UNESCO need to examine which parts of UNESCO are involved in specific activities and how they work together (or not) in specific cases. When governments, the press, or local artists use the acronym UNESCO they also rarely specify the UNESCO actors to which they refer.

My own experience with UNESCO was most intense between 1997 and 2005, when I was President and later Secretary General of the International Council for Traditional Music (ICTM), an international professional organization that was in what was called "formal consultative relations with UNESCO." I was also the editor of the ICTM/UNESCO CD series for a time. As Secretary General, I was in charge of coordinating the scientific and technical evaluations of the

Masterpieces nominations of musical traditions for 2003 and 2005. I saw the nomination files, edited and signed the evaluations by specialists of over fifty nominations, and attended the International Jury meetings as a nonvoting NGO observer.[1] I have followed some of the cultural activities since, especially in the area of intangible cultural heritage. Here is my NGO-based view of UNESCO.[2]

The Components of UNESCO

The United Nations Educational, Scientific, and Cultural Organization (UNESCO) is a very large and complex institution with 195 member states, hundreds of affiliated advisory nongovernmental organizations (NGOs), an often overextended and undersupported professional staff of about two thousand, a central headquarters in Paris, about sixty-five field offices and institutes, National Commissions in almost every country, and "instruments" or agreements that have a profound effect on educational, scientific, and cultural policies in many countries. The most important recent conventions in the area of culture have been on intangible cultural heritage and cultural diversity.[3] UNESCO's huge multilingual and multimedia website is helpful but somewhat difficult to navigate: http://www.unesco.org.

The reason I mention member states first in my description is that the member nations of UNESCO ultimately decide its policies and provide the funding for the organization. The countries do not contribute equal amounts. The United States, when it is a member and paying its assessment, funds the largest percentage of the budget, about 22 percent. Along with Japan (assessed at 15 percent), Germany (8 percent), and France (6 percent), over 50 percent of the budget comes from these four countries. But every country has an equal vote in the biennial General Conference to decide on UNESCO policies and projects and to determine its budget. Many UNESCO programs give priority to regions with the least resources rather than to those that contribute the most.[4] Ultimately the employees of the organization serve and create programs that are of interest to the governments of member states. In my experience, UNESCO does not have a great deal of money to fund specific projects; much of its budget is spent holding meetings where plans are made and wording is hammered out. The actual funding for most cultural activities comes not from the UNESCO budget but from the budgets of each country.[5]

Within the constraints established by the member states and the limited budget at its command, the UNESCO staff, under the leadership of UNESCO's Director-General, develops priorities and assigns proposed budgets to different programs. Almost every biennium has its own priorities.[6] In my experience, many UNESCO staff are overextended—new initiatives are started while earlier ones still require attention—and frustrated by a lack of infrastructural and budgetary support. Like many large organizations, its bureaucracy is complex, its accounting is difficult, and its decision making is often very slow. There can be some conflict between many of the ambitious program builders working to develop new projects and the career support staff that are not always sympathetic to them and the extra work their projects require. This bureaucratic complexity and delay is not unique to UNESCO—they are somewhat similar to my experiences at the Smithsonian Institution and with the Brazilian federal bureaucracy. Any new UNESCO project requires a person extremely capable of working within the bureaucracy and also with the Ambassadors of member states. They also strengthen their cases by enlisting the expertise of affiliated NGOs, which are also an important part of the organization.

Most UNESCO staff members are not subject-matter specialists (there are some very eminent exceptions). Most of them are generalists who consult international networks of specialists when devising their programs. Over three hundred NGOs and a number of foundations have some kind of formal affiliation with UNESCO. International NGOs tend to have international objectives, a diverse executive board with representatives from a wide number of countries, and some kind of national representation in different countries. The association with UNESCO is advisory—the NGOs are not formed by UNESCO, and they have their own objectives, boards, and policies. But they may be called upon by UNESCO for advice in their areas of competence. For example, the ICTM was formally expected to provide expertise in the area of traditional music. Other organizations were responsible for ritual, festival, theater, anthropology, folklore, etc. The ICTM is a member-supported organization whose structure includes a network of National Commissions or liaison officers appointed by the executive board. It supports its activities entirely from member dues and other activities, but because of its status it was able to apply to UNESCO for travel funds for a few scholars to attend its World Conferences who could not otherwise have attended. The ICTM was also regularly invited to send a representative to an annual meeting of NGOs in Paris, at its own expense. At the meeting of UNESCO NGOs I attended in the 1990s, it seemed that the NGOs in health and education were larger and better represented than those in culture. Education and science seemed to be far larger concerns than culture at the time. UNESCO has repeatedly changed its relations with its NGOs and foundations, and this has happened again since my visits in the late 1990s and early 2000s. It is important to remember, however, that official links to subject-matter expertise and international networks of specialists lie in the relations between UNESCO and its affiliated NGOs and foundations.

Although UNESCO is often identified with its iconic (if vastly over-crowded) headquarters in Paris, its employees also work in the sixty-five field offices. These can largely be divided into what are called "cluster offices" that serve several adjacent nations and "national offices" that only serve one country, although there are some other types (for a complete list see http://www.unesco.org/new/en/bfc/all-offices/). The staff in the field offices works with the National Commissions and helps the different nations take advantage of UNESCO initiatives that might prove to be useful to them. Africa has long been a priority area for UNESCO, and the involvement of members of a field office in selecting and preparing the complex nomination paperwork for the Vimbuza healing dance described by Lisa Gilman is part of their job. Members of field offices can also be appointed to serve on National Commissions. Some of their staff members are very well trained and actively engaged in stimulating projects related to UNESCO programs. Similarly, Leah Lowthorp describes the direct involvement of the New Delhi regional office in the Kutiyattam project.

An additional important component of UNESCO, at times essential for the development and forwarding of plans to the main office, is its National Commissions. National Commissions are committees whose members are appointed by the government of each nation that act as liaisons between national governments or organizations and UNESCO (http://unesdoc.unesco.org/images/0022/002269/226924e.pdf). UNESCO is the only branch of the United Nations that has affiliated national organizations like this, and they have played very important, if variable, roles in certain cultural activities. Nations often coordinate UNESCO conventions with their own national institutions involved with education, science, and culture, but these institutions are so varied around the world that the same UNESCO "program" may be administered very differently from country to country—even though they are all charged with implementing UNESCO goals and activities.[7]

Here are two examples where NGOs and National Commissions were involved in activities initiated by the Intangible Heritage office. Noriko Aikawa-Faure (2005, 2009) describes the dissatisfaction of nations in Africa and other parts of the world with UNESCO heritage policies that privileged monuments and buildings but did not recognize the importance of other kinds of heritage (later called *intangible cultural heritage*). The first "instrument" developed by UNESCO to address intangible heritage was the 1989 *Recommendation on the Safeguarding of Traditional Culture and Folklore*. Aikawa-Faure describes how the decision came about to develop a new "instrument" that ultimately became the 2003 Convention for the Safeguarding of the Intangible Cultural Heritage (conventions are more powerful than recommendations—they are binding on the countries that sign them). In her 2009 essay she described the process in considerable detail. First, the Intangible Cultural Heritage unit of UNESCO convened eight regional conferences to discuss the earlier recommendation and intangible cultural heritage (summarized in Seeger 2001) in eight different countries representing regions (Czech Republic, Mexico, Japan, Finland, Uzbekistan, Ghana, New Caledonia, and Lebanon). The participants from each nation attending the conference were selected by their country's National Commission. Representatives of certain international NGOs were also invited by the UNESCO office to participate. These meetings extended over a period of four years. Following those regional meetings a "Global Assessment" meeting was held at the Smithsonian Institution in Washington, DC, hosted by the Center for Folklife and Cultural Heritage.

A second example of roles assigned to National Commissions and NGOs was the nomination process for the Masterpieces of the Intangible Cultural Heritage. Nominations of proposed "masterpieces of intangible cultural heritage" had to be submitted to UNESCO for evaluation by a country's National Commission. The Commissions could only submit one nomination every two years. After a review by UNESCO staff to be sure it was complete, each nomination required a "technical and scientific review" by one or more of the appropriate UNESCO NGOs (described in Seeger 2009). This may have favored proposals by communities having some kind of connection with the

National Commissions—or at least whose supporters had contacts
there. The National Commissions were gatekeepers in this program;
the NGOs made recommendations to an International Jury that met
in Paris and decided what nominations to forward to the Director-
General to proclaim as Masterpieces.

The National Commissions and the member states enjoy a relatively high degree of autonomy from UNESCO headquarters in Paris.
UNESCO can make recommendations, offer training or technical
assistance, and sometimes provide funding, but it cannot interfere
with the internal operations of its member nations. This became particularly clear to me with respect to the action plans submitted with
the nominations of items of intangible cultural heritage for the Masterpieces program, and I am pretty sure it continues to this day with the
nominations to the "Representative Lists" of the 2003 Convention.
The only influence Intangible Cultural Heritage unit staff seemed to
have on the implementation of the action plans was when UNESCO
funded them. Otherwise, nations decided on the policies and often
did not fully fund the action plans they had submitted. The contrast
between the honor of being elected to the Representative List and the
tangible rewards to local tradition-bearers has often been quite large,
as several authors mention here.

The Components of UNESCO and the
Contributions in This Volume

Lisa Gilman's detailed essay on the Vimbuza dance and healing ritual
in Malawi, proclaimed as a Masterpiece of the Oral and Intangible
Heritage in 2005 and now on the Representative List, is a good example of the involvement of several parts of UNESCO. She reports
that the Senior Program Officer of the Malawi National Commission
"contributed to the nomination process." Similar to some other cases I
am familiar with, one of the reasons this form was chosen was because
there was already sufficient information about the dance and ritual
to enable the preparation of the large nomination dossier that had to
be submitted to the Paris office of UNESCO by a certain deadline. It
would have been difficult to start from scratch with a form of heritage
with little prior attention and study. UNESCO deadlines are always
tight and the application requirements for the Masterpieces program
were exigent and extensive—many questions required detailed answers

in a specific order, outlined in a special candidature brochure provided by the Paris office.

Many nations had difficulty assembling all of the required documentation. Gilman was fortunate to be able to see the application. Very often these documents are not made available to researchers or the public. The action plan for safeguarding Vimbuza was prepared by the local Field Office of UNESCO and "the government," and a number of earlier steps were carried out between 2007 and 2009 with funding awarded directly by the UNESCO Intangible Cultural Heritage office in Paris, using funds granted to the program by Japan. Gilman discovered that most people in the rural areas had never heard of UNESCO and were puzzled at the choice of Vimbuza. UNESCO is certainly better known in national capitals and by government bureaucrats than by the general population in most countries, and local residents would not be familiar with the difficulty of the application process that may have guided the selection of Vimbuza. Gilman provides really helpful and rarely available information on the different perspectives on whether the UNESCO listing and funding had been beneficial. She argues that the process in Malawi was from the top down, and the important decisions were made at the national level. In my experience this was often but not always the case. There were a few good examples of "bottom up" projects among the Masterpiece nominations. What is needed, however, is an unusual alliance between motivated local populations and literate specialists who are able to write a successful proposal.

Michael Dylan Foster's essay on the Toshidon ritual reveals a rather different situation from that of Malawi. Members of the local community were somewhat familiar with UNESCO, and the nomination was exciting and important to them. They were thrilled by the selection but concerned about the effects of policies on the informality of Toshidon. Unlike the single Vimbuza dance and ritual that could be proclaimed as a Masterpiece in 2005, Toshidon was one of thirteen ICH elements from Japan entered on the Representative List in 2009. The ability to nominate multiple forms to the Representative List created by the 2003 Convention made it possible for countries to avoid singling out one form and somewhat reduced the apparently arbitrary nature of the selection process described by Gilman in the Vimbuza case. Foster does not provide information about the involvement of the UNESCO National Commission or the UNESCO Field Office, and it appears that the nomination was entirely managed by the Japanese Agency for Cultural Affairs. Japan would not have received any money from UNESCO for undertaking its action plans. While the local residents refer to "UNESCO," in their case the relevant agencies were actually those of the Japanese government and entrepreneurs involved in tourism. UNESCO, as such, was only involved when the nomination was voted to the List at the 2009 meeting of the nation-states signers of the 2003 Convention. UNESCO as a brand, or "floating signifier," may be important within Japan, but UNESCO as a policy-making body has very little direct influence on Japanese cultural heritage policy, which has its own very long and important history dating back at least to 1950 (Arisawa 2012). Foster's conclusion, that there are many different UNESCOs, anticipates my own general point: it is difficult to pinpoint a single "UNESCO" given its many different constituent parts.

Carol Silverman's essay on the failed nominations of the Macedonian Teškoto dance reveals the difficulty culture workers in some countries have had in preparing documents that meet all the requirements of the UNESCO ICH guidelines. It is not clear whether the Macedonian authors of the nominations had UNESCO technical assistance in preparing the nominations. Macedonia nominated the dance for the 2003 and 2005 rounds of the Masterpieces project, but Silverman is probably correct in suggesting that the language of the nomination dossiers, the omission of mention of the Roma minority groups normally employed as musicians, and other features of the dossiers hindered the dance's approval by the International Jury that made the final decisions on the nominations (the nomination and selection process is described in Seeger 2009). Communications between national cultural organizations and the Paris office of UNESCO sometimes resulted in misunderstandings and incomplete or flawed applications for UNESCO designations.

Leah Lowthorp's description of the aftermath of the UNESCO proclamation of the Kutiyattam of Kerala as a Masterpiece in 2001 (the first Proclamation of the Masterpieces project at UNESCO) focuses on the aftermath of the implementation of the action plan. Her case reveals the continued involvement of the New Delhi office of UNESCO in the action plan, which was not always the case. The essay is richly detailed and reveals important aspects of the impact of the implementation of action plans. Her discussion of the UNESCO "toolbox" is important, because much seems to remain the same while other things have changed. Comparing the 1989 Recommendations on Folklore with the 2003 Convention, one can see some profound differences as well as some similarities. The statement in the Convention that there is no fixed, authentic form to most ICH was a hard-fought wording supported by ethnomusicologists and anthropologists but resisted by nonacademics more accustomed to using "authentic" and "original." Committees consisting of representatives of NGOs and nation-states debated the wording of the convention for many weeks. The final wording was often a mixture of various positions, especially in the definitions. The more significant the document, the more contentious and difficult the wording. Readers of the 2003 Convention may well puzzle over the lengthy definitions and the detailed listing of what is and is not included. Each word may be extremely important to one group or another. This is why the toolkit can be described as both the same and different—both old and new elements are there.

China has been extremely active in the area of ICH for a number of reasons and the country has a tendency toward top-down cultural policies (though not always; see Rees 2012). The nomination process to the local, provincial, and national lists, as well as nomination to the UNESCO Representative Lists, is quite complex and has left many groups of artists puzzled, resentful, and in conflict with one another. Here again, these decisions are not UNESCO's but rather the specific implementation of cultural policy by government agencies. Ziying You's observation that the effects of ICH policies can disempower local communities and people is a very important lesson to take away from this case, though in some of the other cases (Malawi and Japan) that does not seem to have occurred uniformly. The unhappiness of local artists about not receiving much money from their collaboration with ICH projects is not unique to China. It has been reported in many other countries, among them the shamans on Cheju Island, South Korea.

Kyoim Yun's essay addresses the impact on local shamans of inscription in the Representative List and raises important issues of the moral, intellectual, and practical implications of UNESCO policies on an island province that has received three different designations—as a World Heritage Site, as a Bioreserve, and, most recently, as the site of an element of intangible cultural heritage that has been inscribed on the Representative List. Her essay describes a complex situation.

It appears to me that the problems described stem from the South Korean decision to propose to nominate shamanism to the Representative List, which does not seem to have been suggested by a UNESCO unit. South Korea had a very elaborate system for preserving cultural heritage long before the UNESCO Convention, one that has been discussed by Keith Howard (2012). The failure of attempts to make this form of South Korean shamanism a tourist spectacle is an important caution to those who conflate UNESCO lists with income from hordes of wealthy tourists.

Conclusion

The case studies presented in this edited collection are all extremely valuable for the ethnographic perspectives they provide on local perceptions about elements of ICH that have been nominated to the UNESCO Lists. Each also contributes thoughtful reflections on intangible cultural heritage in general. My contribution to this has been an attempt to show how the results attributed to UNESCO are in fact influenced to different degrees by central UNESCO policies, the participation of NGOs, the actions of National Commissions, and the cultural policies of each country. Because UNESCO has so many components it can be difficult to figure out why things happen the way they do. Our ethnographies need to be as attuned to the specifics of what part of UNESCO (and even what individuals within them) we refer to as they are to what different members of local communities think about the effects of UNESCO-attributed policies on their own lives. The cultural policies of most of the countries in the world have been profoundly influenced by UNESCO, but not all in the same way. This can lead to significant differences "on the ground."

Notes

1. The documents relating to the evaluations of the Masterpieces nominations are confidential, though I make some general references to them here. Participants in the selection were told we could discuss nominations that were approved but asked to respect the member states of those that were not approved by not discussing the deliberations about their nominations.

2. I am very grateful to ICTM Secretary General Dieter Christensen and ICTM Board Members Krister Malm and Wim Van Zanten for their perspec-

tives on UNESCO over the years, but they are not to blame for any errors in my presentation.

3. The UNESCO Convention on the Protection and Promotion of the Diversity of Cultural Expressions was passed in 2005 and emphasizes the right of states to "protect and promote diversity of cultural expressions" (UNESCO 2005).

4. This is quite different from US politics and may be the source of some of the frustration of US governmental bodies with UNESCO. The largest donor, in this case, does not get any necessary advantage in policy making.

5. An exception to this general statement was the funding made available to some countries to enable them to prepare their plans to safeguard the heritage that had been proclaimed a Masterpiece of the Oral and Intangible Heritage. Two essays correctly mention direct funding from UNESCO, which was sometimes granted to countries that could not afford to implement their action plans. But the entire Masterpieces program was funded by "extra budgetary" money (a targeted donation) from Japan. UNESCO more often adds a piece of tangible, intangible, or natural heritage to the representative list and then expects the nations themselves to support its safeguarding.

6. For the draft plan for 2014–17 see http://unesdoc.unesco.org/images/0022/002200/220074e.pdf.

7. An example of these differences is that the ministry of culture in some countries is also responsible for tourism, while in others culture may be part of the ministry of education or combined with sports. The potential for tourism has never been a selection criterion for UNESCO safeguarding. Proposals that highlighted the benefits of tourism were not well received in the Masterpieces nominations, partly because the impact of tourism is not necessarily beneficial. But there is no question that tourism is on the minds of national, regional, and municipal leaders, as well as performers themselves. In some cases, however, the imagined hordes of tourists do not appear, as Kyoim Yun describes in this volume.

References Cited

Aikawa-Faure, Noriko. 2005. Video Interview with Noriko Aikawa-Faure. In *Second Proclamation of the Masterpieces of the Oral and Intangible Heritage of Humanity*. Compact disc. Paris: UNESCO Intangible Heritage Section.

———. 2009. "From the Proclamation of Masterpieces to the *Convention for the Safeguarding of Intangible Cultural Heritage*." In *Intangible Heritage*, edited by Laurajane Smith and Natsuko Akagawa, 13–44. New York: Routledge.

Arisawa, Shino. 2012. "Dichotomies between 'Classical' and 'Folk' in the Intangible Cultural Properties of Japan." In *Music as Intangible Cultural Heritage: Policy, Ideology, and Practice in the Preservation of East Asian Traditions*, edited by Keith Howard, 182–95. Farnham, Surrey, UK: Ashgate.

Howard, Keith, ed. 2012. *Music as Intangible Cultural Heritage: Policy, Ideology, and Practice in the Preservation of East Asian Traditions*. Farnham, Surrey, UK: Ashgate.

Rees, Helen. 2012. "Intangible Cultural Heritage in China Today: Policy and Practice in the Early 21st Century." In *Music as Intangible Cultural Heritage:*

Policy, Ideology, and Practice in the Preservation of East Asian Traditions, edited by Keith Howard, 23–54. Farnham, Surrey, UK: Ashgate.

Seeger, Anthony. 2001. "Summary Report on the Regional Seminars." In *Safeguarding Traditional Cultures: A Global Assessment*, edited by Peter Seitel, 36–41. Washington, DC: Smithsonian Center for Folklife and Cultural Heritage.

———. 2009. "Lessons Learned from the ICTM (NGO) Evaluation of Nominations for the UNESCO Masterpieces of the Oral and Intangible Heritage of Humanity, 2001–2005." In *Intangible Heritage*, edited by Laurajane Smith and Natsuko Akagawa, 112–28. London: Routledge.

UNESCO. 2005. Convention on the Protection and Promotion of the Diversity of Cultural Expressions. Paris: UNESCO. http://portal.unesco.org/en/ev.php -URL_ID=31038&URL_DO=DO_TOPIC&URL_SECTION=201.html.

ANTHONY SEEGER is Distinguished Professor of Ethnomusicology, Emeritus, at the University of California, Los Angeles, and Director Emeritus of Smithsonian Folkways Recordings. He served as President (1997–99) and Secretary General (2001–5) of the International Council for Traditional Music, an NGO in formal consultative relations with UNESCO. He is currently a Research Associate at the Smithsonian Institution's Center for Folklife Programs and Cultural Heritage.

8 Learning to Live with ICH: Diagnosis and Treatment

Prologue. At the doctor's office.

Patient: "What is it, doctor?"

Doctor: "There's no easy way to break this to you: you have heritage."

Patient: "Heritage? Are you serious? What kind?"

Doctor: "Intangible. I'm sorry."

Patient: "Intangible heritage . . . How bad is it?"

Doctor: "It is in urgent need of safeguarding. It's already metacultural."

Patient: "What's the prognosis?"

Doctor: "Intangible heritage is chronic, I'm afraid. It is often terminal, but in your case there is reason to be optimistic. You can live with your heritage for a long time to come, provided we take immediate measures to safeguard it."

Patient: "Will it be painful?"

Doctor: "I won't lie to you. The treatment is not pleasant. You will have to learn to relate differently to yourself and to your heritage from here on out."

Patient: "Shouldn't we get a second opinion?"

Doctor: "I recommend contacting UNESCO. If they agree with the diagnosis, we might get you on their list."

Patient: "Would that help?"

Doctor: "If you're listed, UNESCO can help document your heritage, identify its elements, analyze the mode of transmission, raise awareness, even draw up a five-year safeguarding plan."

Patient: "Is all that really necessary?"

Doctor: "Without proper treatment, I'm afraid your heritage may lose what authenticity it has left. Worst case scenario, you might be looking at a full-blown case of fakelore."

Patient: "Wait a minute. That's what they said when our parents' generation came down with tradition. But they beat that."

Doctor: "They did, with a lot of drugs. But back in those days, tradition responded to drugs. Intangible heritage is more serious. And it is highly communicable. We haven't found an effective way to contain it yet."

Enter UNESCO

The Meaning of Intangible Heritage: An Empirical Approach

In his *Philosophical Investigations*, Ludwig Wittgenstein (2009, 43) argues that "the meaning of a word is its use in the language." In other words, Wittgenstein suggests, if we want to learn what a word means or how a sign signifies, we cannot rely on formal definitions; they are a dead end. Furthermore, it is fruitless to examine the external signifier to which our word points, and etymology will not help us grasp its meaning. Rather, the question of meaning is empirical. The only way to discover the meaning of a word is to go into the field, to observe how it is used in language.

That is the task that the authors in this volume have set for themselves with reference to intangible heritage. What they present are empirically grounded and theoretically informed studies of the meaning of intangible heritage at the local level, in the field. Based on the authors' extensive fieldwork, each essay gives a detailed, grounded understanding of the implementation of UNESCO's 2003 intangible heritage convention, bringing out the conflicting perspectives and different voices of practitioners, administrators, and local populations. Their analyses are always nuanced and very often enlightening. Taken together, the essays go a long way toward bringing out the meaning of intangible heritage: its use on the ground. The edited collection is therefore a most welcome addition to the fast-growing literature on intangible heritage.

Intangible Heritage as Diagnosis

In her essay in this volume, Lisa Gilman explores the process and implications of inscribing the Vimbuza healing dance from Malawi on UNESCO's Representative List of the Intangible Cultural Heritage of Humanity. Vimbuza was in many ways an odd candidate; expediency seems to have been the principal motivation for its inscription—it was already well documented, which made it easier to compile a dossier for its nomination. As Gilman makes clear, however, the local practitioners of Vimbuza by and large do not regard it as heritage, nor even as a cultural practice. For them, it is a medical practice: Vimbuza names a disease and it names the cure; by means of traditional rituals, Vimbuza healers diagnose and treat spirit-related illnesses.

It is not hard to see why Gilman's healers feel that the concept of heritage misrepresents their healing practices; the label fits about as comfortably as a Procrustean bed. As Gilman shows, the translation of the ritual into intangible heritage robs it of its powers and its substance, leaving only the dance as a form of display, with the ritual experts going through the motions and acting as if for an audience that is not looking to be healed but rather just looking. To invoke Barbara Kirshenblatt-Gimblett (1995, 1998), heritage cultivates a metacultural relationship to practice, but it is evident here that the metacultural relationship comes at the expense of the preexisting relation to the practice, which is medical. It stands to reason, therefore, that those Malawians who would prefer to eradicate Vimbuza seem more favorably disposed to its standing as intangible heritage than do many of its practitioners.

Reading the five other fine case studies in this volume on intangible heritage, I kept referring back to Gilman's analysis of Vimbuza. The parallels in the other five case studies are often quite striking: the sweeping social changes cited as evidence of the need for safeguarding, the actual measures taken to safeguard the practices in question, and the intended and unintended outcomes that the authors identify. Vimbuza is in many ways the anomaly. Yet it seems to me that Vimbuza, in Gilman's presentation, holds a key to understanding the other cases.

It took a couple of readings before it occurred to me; the relationship between Vimbuza and the other five cases is in fact inverted. If it is certainly true that *intangible heritage*, with all that the term entails, is not an apt description of Vimbuza, *Vimbuza* on the other hand describes rather well what intangible heritage is and does. If Vimbuza names an illness "caused by spirits that possess a person, causing a variety of physical and mental ailments" (Gilman, p. 61) intangible heritage may likewise be described as the technical term for a cultural malady brought on by social, economic, and demographic change. If Vimbuza refers also "to the rituals that are used to diagnose and heal these spirit-related illnesses," intangible heritage may then also be described as a diagnosis and safeguarding as a form of treatment. If Vimbuza healers "diagnose and heal spirit-related illnesses" (p. 61), the same may be said, *mutatis mutandis*, of the experts who administer intangible heritage. In this analysis, the people who perform Vimbuza and the people who would safeguard Vimbuza are doing exactly the same thing; ironically, that is why their actions are at cross-purposes.

Reading the other five cases in light of this one, it is plain to see that intangible heritage offers in each case a broad diagnosis of what is wrong. Be it economic development (as in the Korean case), depopulation (as in the cases from Japan and Macedonia), social upheaval (the Indian case), or political persecution (in China), intangible heritage names a cultural condition requiring the metacultural intervention of experts (see table 1).

Thus intangible heritage is, first of all, a diagnosis. It gives a name to a condition that is increasingly common in industrial and postindustrial societies under circumstances of economic, political, technological, and demographic change—for which the shorthand is globalization. Among the symptoms of intangible heritage is a sense of alienation and imperilment. If left untreated, the prognosis is usually endangerment and imminent loss.

Safeguarding as Treatment: Reforming Relationships and Practices

Known as safeguarding, the treatment is a long-term, intensive intervention requiring advanced expertise to obtain the desired results, and its side effects are in many cases worse than the condition itself. Developed by heritage professionals under the auspices of UNESCO, modeled on experimental twentieth-century forms of cultural therapy from Japan and South Korea, the condition of intangible heritage is

Table 1
Intangible Heritage as Diagnosis

INDIA
(Leah Lowthorp, p. 20)

In the course of the twentieth century, the system that had sustained Kutiyattam as an elite, temple-based occupation for nearly one thousand years crumbled beneath the artists' feet in a dramatic tide of change that swept over Kerala and the emerging Indian nation.

KOREA
(Kyoim Yun, p. 52)

Development on the island has taken away many of the jobs of the diving ladies, the ritual's "real owners." . . . On a practical level, most villages no longer have a need to sponsor the ritual, and only a few are now in any way concerned with its practice.

JAPAN
(Michael Dylan Foster, p. 84)

Since Toshidon is child-oriented and there are fewer and fewer children on the island, it is possible that in years to come they will not be able to perform it regularly, if at all. . . . Leaders have calculated that, given current family situations, there may be no children of appropriate age left within the next three or four years.

MACEDONIA
(Carol Silverman, p. 101)

In the late nineteenth century Galičnik had three thousand inhabitants, but during the twentieth century the population declined due to urbanization and migration. After World War II and the socialization of private land, the village lost its economic base; the last wedding was held in 1953, and by the 1960s only a few elderly residents remained.

CHINA
(Ziying You, p. 117)

When the tradition was officially banned during the Cultural Revolution, several villagers from Yangxie practiced it secretly, and some were even sent to prison because of their continued participation.

TABLE 2
Safeguarding as Treatment (Institutions and Genres of Display)

INDIA
(Leah Lowthorp, pp. 22–23)

Kutiyattam's action plan began to be implemented in 2004. . . . The funds were used to support meetings of a Kutiyattam network, the revival of plays, publications, student training, public awareness-raising workshops and performances, academic seminars, the production of ten documentaries, and a workshop. . . . In 2007 it [the Sangeet Natak Akademi] founded a national center, Kutiyattam Kendra, in Kerala's capital city of Trivandrum.

KOREA
(Kyoim Yun, pp. 50–51)

The Association was also mobilized to perform in the National Center for Korean Traditional Performing Arts (NCKTPA) in Seoul. . . . One of the online media blurbs highlighted the advantage of observing the island's ritual without actually going there.

MALAWI
(Lisa Gilman, p. 74)

Since the Convention's ratification, the Department of Culture convened an official body, the National Intangible Cultural Heritage Committee, that comprises cultural workers, academics, and ethnic association members, among others, who now meet regularly to share information and strategies. Additionally, the Department of Culture, together with the local UNESCO Commission, has surveyed ICH elements across the country, documenting cultural practices and stimulating greater interest in and awareness of their value.

generally treated with a combination of social institutions (intangible heritage councils, committees, commissions, networks, foundations, etc.) and expressive genres (intangible heritage lists, festivals, workshops, competitions, prizes, documentaries, promotional materials, etc.), with the former administering the latter in practices that are jointly termed *safeguarding.* When successful, safeguarding (1) *reforms the relationship of subjects with their own practices* (through sentiments such as "pride"), (2) *reforms the practices* (orienting them toward display through various conventional heritage genres), and ultimately

TABLE 2
(*continued*)

JAPAN
(Michael Dylan Foster, p. 82)
Other than signing off on the nomination form, the islanders themselves had no direct involvement with the UNESCO selection; in fact, they only realized the inscription was official when a newspaper reporter from the mainland called the village office to ask how they felt about it.

MACEDONIA
(Carol Silverman, p. 101)

The Galičnik Wedding has become an annual event . . . enacted in a two-day condensed version by members of the Skopje-based Kočo Racin dance ensemble plus several former villagers who formed an association. Currently thousands of people attend, and competitive applications are taken from couples with heritage from Galičnik who want to be married during the ritual. The event is covered by the media and heavily promoted by the ministry of tourism. Political speeches, a song contest, and anniversary celebrations have been added.

CHINA
(Ziying You, p. 125)

It is ironic that the local tradition was "protected" and transmitted primarily by the newly established Hongtong Center for the Safeguarding of ICH instead of by members of the communities who have long practiced it. Of course, the conundrum here is that the Center has not historically contributed to the tradition, but it is now charged with safeguarding it; in contrast, the shè and temple reconstruction associations that have maintained the tradition have no voice in the safeguarding process.

---

(3) *reforms the relationship of the practicing subjects with themselves* (through social institutions of heritage that formalize previously informal relations and centralize previously dispersed powers) (see table 2).

Beginning with the last point, the cases analyzed in this volume offer ample evidence of this reformation of the collective subjects of heritage. From Kutiyattam theater in Kerala, India, to the Galičnik wedding in Macedonia, the heritagization of traditional practices brings into being new social institutions and concentrates in them the power to make decisions that were previously distributed among a number of different social actors or else were simply unthinkable before the practices were framed as intangible heritage. Thus in 2007, for example, a national center, Kutiyattam Kendra, was founded in Kerala's capital to administer a national "action plan" for safeguarding the theatrical tradition. In China, the Hongtong Center for the Safe-guarding of ICH was charged with safeguarding the Hongtong Zouqin Xisu ("the custom of visiting sacred relatives in Hongtong"), and this new center took over many competences previously dispersed among local populations. In Malawi, the Department of Culture has "convened an official body, the National Intangible Cultural Heritage Committee, that comprises cultural workers, academics, and ethnic association members, among others" (Gilman, p. 74). Moreover, Gilman reveals, a special "Vimbuza Healers and Dancers Association of Malawi" has been formed that immediately established a code of conduct for its members with the proclaimed purpose of countering "the negative image of Vimbuza caused by inappropriate practice" (p. 66). In all cases, we are witness to an institutionalization of so-cial relations, a centralization of powers, and the bringing into being of new social actors: centers, councils, associations, committees, com-missions, juries, networks.

This reformation of the subjects of intangible heritage goes hand in hand with a reformation of the objects of intangible heritage: the practices, representations, expressions, knowledge, and skills to which the 2003 Convention refers in its definition. Translation into the language of intangible heritage is subject to generic conventions associated with what we might term the *intangible heritage genres*. These genres promote the practices, representations, etc., and in the process they orient them toward display. Thus, for example, Leah Lowthorp (p. 22) mentions among the items on the action plan for safeguarding Kutiyattam: "publications, student training, public awareness-raising workshops and performances, academic seminars, the production of ten documentaries," and so on. As theater, Kutiyattam is already versed in display, of course, but the action plan diversifies its modes of presentation. In comparison, the safeguarding plan for Vimbuza in Malawi includes, in addition to the formation of an association and the establishment of a code of conduct, a new book about Vimbuza by a professor at Mzuzu University and a museum exhibit about Vimbuza in the Mzuzu Museum, an inventory of Vimbuza practitioners, and the regular organization of Vimbuza dance festivals. The festival is a genre of display particularly closely associated with the safeguarding of intangible heritage; so much so, in fact, that in Malawi an illness and a medical practice for its treatment have been festivalized. Gilman (p. 68) cites Malawi healer Lestina Makwakwa who was, like many of her colleagues, "especially critical of the idea of a Vimbuza festival, which was part of the safeguarding plan that followed the UNESCO designation, or other events in which Vimbuza would be performed outside of its ritual context, because these displays strip it of its significance."

Promotion and awareness-raising carry various implications for the practices recognized as intangible heritage. Thus one observes in many cases their condensation as a condition for their transportability outside community boundaries, whether literally through traveling performances (which are surprisingly common), virtually through their mediatization, or socially through the inclusion of tourists as spectators. In Galičnik in Macedonia, a traditional village wedding ceremony that used to be up to eight days long is enacted as a staged recreation in a two-day condensed version over a weekend, with thousands of people in attendance, an event that is "heavily promoted by the Ministry of Tourism" (Silverman, p. 101) and extensively covered by the media, although it failed in its bid for UNESCO recognition. On a related note, as Yun reports, once the Yŏngdŭng Rite had been inscribed on UNESCO's Representative List in 2009, shamans from Cheju Island were mobilized to stage the ritual for a cosmopolitan audience in Seoul. One of the media blurbs for the event even "highlighted the advantage of observing the island's ritual without actually going there" (Yun, p. 51). At another similar occasion, a heritage promotion event at the Cheju Art Center, Kim, one of the shamans whom Yun interviewed, complains that the organizers "kept requesting that the ritual be shortened to fit the time frame for the whole event," and in the end they were "pushed to perform for twenty minutes total, a situation Kim compared with abbreviating Shakespeare's play *Romeo and Juliet* to four words, 'Oh Romeo!' 'Oh Juliet!'" (p. 50).

Compensation is another striking feature of measures taken to safeguard intangible heritage, more common even than the condensation characteristic of its genres of display. The case studies in this volume, all save the one from Malawi, testify to the compensatory function of safeguarding. Reading them all at once, one cannot help but notice how safeguarding always compensates (or attempts to do so) for the change in social and economic circumstances that creates the condition diagnosed as intangible heritage. Thus safeguarding often replaces previous modes of administration with state patronage, as in the cases of Kutiyattam theater in Kerala and the custom of visiting sacred relatives in Hongtong. Moreover, it substitutes tourists and other spectators for local participants, as in the cases of the diving women in the Yŏngdŭng Rite on Cheju Island and the children in Toshidon on the island of Shimo-Koshikijima. The same holds true for the villagers in Galičnik and neighboring villages, replaced by foreign tourists and spectators from the city, even though in this particular case the local diagnosis of intangible heritage has not been upheld by UNESCO's "second opinion." The Malawi case is again the exception that proves the rule, as the Vimbuza ritual, a popular medical practice in great demand, is actually in no need of safeguarding and especially not of compensatory remediation—neither state patronage nor the substitution of spectators for local participants; in fact, through Gilman's analysis safeguarding emerges as the single greatest threat to its continued practice.

Taken together, the case studies in this volume also offer insight into the ways in which safeguarding cultivates and changes the relationship of practitioners and local populations with their practices (see table 3). It is particularly interesting to see how they reveal the common emotional register of intangible heritage. Recognition by UNESCO and national authorities, we find, very often elicits a response that people themselves describe variously as pride, confidence, self-respect, or self-belief. Thus in Kutiyattam theater, the greatest effect of the recognition bestowed by UNESCO, according to one of the practitioners whom Leah Lowthorp quotes, "was that working artists had an awakening, they found a belief in themselves." He adds: "Now we're really proud to be in Kutiyattam. It has gained value" (Lowthorp, p. 27). In a similar vein, the selection of Toshidon for UNESCO's Representative List is, according to one of Foster's informants on the island, not "a point of 'pride' but rather . . . a reason for 'confidence' or *jishin* . . . [that] implies a deep sense that what one is doing has meaning" (Foster, p. 89).

TABLE 3
Safeguarding as Treatment (Effects)

INDIA
(Leah Lowthorp, p. 27)

The greatest impact this wider social recognition has had is upon the way many artists relate to their art. As one artist poignantly expressed: "The greatest effect was that working artists had an awakening, they found a belief in themselves. That was the *greatest*. Now we're really proud to be in Kutiyattam. It has gained value. When we go to programs we are happy, because everyone doesn't see us as unimportant anymore. They see us and treat us with respect. . . . Our respect grew."

KOREA
(Kyoim Yun, pp. 47, 54–55

Immediately after the ritual's inscription on the Representative List, all concerned parties seemed to revel in the global recognition.

The ritual's global recognition strips the shamans and their clients of the option to cease the ritual, which many seashore villages on Cheju have already done. Although the incumbent skill holder has reached the pinnacle of his profession, the Association's office manager pointed out, future generations of the Association will feel it even more burdensome to maintain the public event.

JAPAN
(Michael Dylan Foster, pp. 88–89, 84)

One island friend described the selection not as a point of "pride" but rather as a reason for "confidence" or jishin. . . . The word jishin might be literally translated as "self belief," and implies a deep sense that what one is doing has meaning.

He and others have "internalized" the recognition and feel a certain "burden" because of Toshidon's newfound global status. . . . This "burden" . . . is manifest as an increased sense of responsibility for the future of the tradition. . . . Some residents feel UNESCO recognition compels them to keep the tradition alive in some form.

MACEDONIA
(Carol Silverman, p. 106)

They wanted to convince the audience that if UNESCO valued Kopačka, then we all should. They were clearly proud. . . . Dramče villagers employ the discourse of UNESCO in part because they have been trained to present Kopačka to outsiders by ICH workers both from their village association and from the Ministry of Culture; they have also learned to objectify and label their dance and to verbally express pride in their heritage.

Safeguarding as Treatment: Pride, Confidence, Harmony

In 2008, when presenting the first Representative List of the Intangible Cultural Heritage of Humanity, Koïchiro Matsuura, UNESCO's Director-General, declared his confidence that "with time, this List—designed to give more visibility to our living heritage—will contribute to raising awareness of its importance and instill a sense of pride and belonging to custodian communities" (UNESCO 2008). The prestige of international recognition that comes with listing is thus designed to elicit the self-recognition of communities as the inheritors and custodians of their own heritage. It is supposed to induce in people a desire to have a heritage and to take care of it; to curate their own practices, or those of other segments of the local population.

The president of UNESCO's first jury for the List of Masterpieces of the Oral and Intangible Heritage of Humanity (the predecessor of the Representative List), Spanish author, dissident, and Nobel laureate Juan Goytisolo, spearheaded an effort in the second half of the 1990s to protect Jemaa el-Fna, a busy, dynamic marketplace in Marrakesh that is the site of myriad performances—storytelling, snake-charming, fortune-telling, dental care, preaching, and pickpocketing, to name a few. At the time, the city and its contractors were planning to get rid of the marketplace and kick out the peddlers and performers to make way for a shopping mall and a parking lot. Goytisolo and likeminded intellectuals in Marrakesh enlisted the aid of UNESCO and its "critical gaze" (to quote Foster's felicitous phrase, p. 89) to save Jemaa el-Fna. In Goytisolo's analysis, the key to saving the square was to change the relationship of the local population (in particular its wealthier, more powerful elements) to Jemaa el-Fna:

> The bourgeois "society" of Marrakesh looks at the square with disdain and has on various occasions attempted to do away with it because they think it is a symbol of backwardness and decay. . . . Well, what we are attempting—and UNESCO's decision will help us in this—is to change the way that many of Marrakesh's own inhabitants look at the square. So that they feel a justified sense of pride. (Espada 2004; my translation)

There is nothing unusual about the disdain of the Marrakesh bourgeoisie for Jemaa el-Fna: "Often," Goytisolo continues, "it is the alien gaze that returns beauty and integrity to places. Alhambra, for example, was discovered by English writers and travelers. Borrow recounts that when he asked people from Granada about Alhambra they referred to it as 'these little Moor things.' Something similar is happening in Marrakesh."

Through this "alien gaze," and by means of the social institutions and genres of display characteristic of intangible heritage, Jemaa el-Fna is symbolically reformed from a rogue element to a public theater of power and Marrakesh-ness. Existing customs, habits, pastimes, and expressions are transformed, as Kirshenblatt-Gimblett (1998) would have it, to representations of themselves, as they become objects of safeguarding through plans and policies developed by local, national, and international experts with reference to the Intangible Cultural Heritage Convention.

With recognition, then, and with the self-recognition it elicits, comes a duty to safeguard one's own practices. In this volume, Yun and Foster throw a fascinating light on the onerous sense of responsibility to which this may give rise. Foster's study of Toshidon masking traditions on the remote Japanese island of Shimo-Koshikijima and Yun's study of shamanic ritual tradition on Cheju Island in Korea's southern sea are both set against the background of dramatic social changes, spurred on by depopulation on the one hand and economic development on the other. In both cases these transformations have all but eliminated the traditional audience for these rites and their very raison d'être: within a few years, there will be no children left of the appropriate age for whom to perform Toshidon, and the diving ladies in Cheju, the "real owners" of the shamanic ritual, have lost their jobs and are therefore no longer in need of the shamans' services.

Having internalized the global recognition of their traditions, Foster's informants "feel a certain 'burden'" and "an increased sense of responsibility for the future of the tradition," to the extent even that UNESCO's recognition "compels them to keep the tradition alive in some form"—despite the fact that there soon will be no more children on the island for whom to perform it. Yun adds that perhaps the most important effect of UNESCO's recognition in Cheju Island is that it "strips the shamans and their clients of the option to cease the ritual, which many seashore villages on Cheju have already done." When it comes right down to it, that is what safeguarding living, intangible heritage entails. Curiously, the alternative to safeguarding heritage is never not to safeguard heritage; the alternative to safeguarding heritage is always to destroy it (Poulot 2006, 157). The discourse of heritage frames safeguarding in ethical terms; once we accept the subject position this discourse has devised for us, we have severely limited the choice of verbs with which it makes any sense for us to act on our heritage. We may choose between the synonyms of safeguarding (preserve, promote, transmit, celebrate, etc.).

Safeguarding as Treatment: Protection as Dispossession

As Leah Lowthorp explains, considerable funds have been invested in safeguarding Kutiyattam as a result of its UNESCO listing. Among other things, this has meant, in the words of one of the artists with whom Lowthorp worked in Kerala, that "Kutiyattam became a profession with a salary base. . . . Ramesh was able to marry, because he could say he works here. That's a real social change." The funds come with strings attached, however. They are disbursed through institutions, and artists who are lucky enough to earn a salary are now "required to reside at their institution six days per week, to formally request time off thereby reducing their salary, to take attendance for both students and artists, and to submit paperwork detailing their monthly activities" (Lowthorp, p. 29). Another artist whom Lowthorp spoke with reflects: "Now we have a condition of normal working people. It is good for an office but bad for art."

If intangible heritage is a diagnosis and safeguarding is the treatment, it is not without its side effects (see table 4). Some of the case studies in this collection give warning that the side effects may sometimes be worse than the condition. Thus You concludes from her study of the ramifications of UNESCO's recognition of the custom of visiting sacred relatives in Hongtong that "attempts at safeguarding ICH in Hongtong have caused a series of transformations that disempower local communities and people" (You, p. 124).

Lowthorp and You are not alone in drawing such conclusions. Various other studies signal in the same general direction (e.g., Noyes 2006; Foster 2011; Hafstein 2012, 2014; Lowthorp 2013; Kapchan 2014; Silverman 2014). They live in many different places in different parts of the world, but they share the same complaint: that as part of the safeguarding of intangible heritage local actors are asked to surrender to experts and councils and administrators the control over their own cultural practices. Which raises the question: is that, ultimately, the meaning (in Wittgenstein's sense) of intangible heritage? Is safeguarding dispossession by another name? To be constructive, perhaps

TABLE 4
Safeguarding as Treatment (Side Effects)

INDIA
(Leah Lowthorp, pp. 29–30)

While the previous model left day-to-day practices largely unregulated, artists became required to reside at their institution six days per week, to formally request time off thereby reducing their salary, to take attendance for both students and artists, and to submit paperwork detailing their monthly activities. . . . This overall process was perceived by many as a loss of freedom. One artist reflected: "We were totally free with our programs but now that has all been regulated. Now we have a condition of normal working people. It is good for an office but bad for art."

KOREA
(Kyoim Yun, p. 50)

The staff kept requesting that the ritual be shortened to fit the time frame for the whole event, a demand hardly new for staged performances. In the end, simbang were pushed to perform for twenty minutes total, a situation Kim compared with abbreviating Shakespeare's play *Romeo and Juliet* to four words: "Oh, Romeo! Oh, Juliet!" From his view, it was nearly impossible to show anything meaningful from the daylong ritual in such a short time and thus compromised the shamans' mission of displaying the authentic tradition anticipated by the audience. In such a show, he said straightforwardly, simbang are "used as commodities."

MALAWI
(Lisa Gilman, p. 68–69)

She was especially critical of the idea of a Vimbuza festival, which was part of the safeguarding plan that followed the UNESCO designation, or other events in which Vimbuza would be performed outside of its ritual context, because these displays strip it of its significance. . . . Those afflicted with Vimbuza could not entertain because while "dancing" they would not have control over themselves. . . . Healers Gondwe and Luhanga similarly explained that they felt that these performers were making fun of Vimbuza.

JAPAN
(Michael Dylan Foster, p. 85–86)

The Motomachi preservation society was conscious of treading a delicate line between inclusivity and the maintenance of what it considered the integrity and effectiveness of Toshidon; in the end, they decided to open the ritual on a limited basis—so that visitors might be accommodated but events would not be disrupted.

TABLE 4
(*continued*)

CHINA
(Ziying You, pp. 121–22, 124)

The ICH application had fueled local conflicts between the communities, and it was hard for them to reach any agreement. . . . The local conflicts among Yangxie, Lishan, and Wan'an did not originate during the ICH application but they were exacerbated in the process.

My case study reveals a similar process: attempts at safeguarding ICH in Hongtong County have caused a series of transformations that disempower local communities and people.

---

we might instead ask: where and under what circumstances is safeguarding not a means of dispossession? What conditions must it fulfill?

Intangible Heritage: Epidemiology

As the prologue's doctor noted, intangible heritage is spreading fast: the condition, the diagnosis, and the treatment. At the time of writing, UNESCO has recognized 327 elements of the intangible heritage of humanity, and the numbers rise every year. That list is merely representative, however. At the national level, the numbers are far higher. National inventories of intangible heritage each identify elements in the dozens or hundreds, depending on the country. At the time of writing, for example, Switzerland alone (population 8 million) officially recognizes 167 elements of intangible heritage, while Peru (population 30 million) recognizes some 150 elements, and India (population 1.21 billion) recognizes 34.

Unconfirmed cases of intangible heritage are potentially far more numerous. Thus at a meeting I observed in UNESCO headquarters in Paris in June 2003, a Japanese diplomat claimed that "in my country alone it is said that there are more than sixty thousand items of intangible cultural heritage" (Hafstein 2009, 103). On the other hand, at a UNESCO meeting in Algiers in 2006, I witnessed a diplomat from Luxembourg claiming (straight-faced) that there is only one intangible heritage in his country; hence it was imperative that the heritage be listed and safeguarded, he continued, lest the people of Luxembourg be left with none.

As may be surmised from this last pair of numbers, an epidemiology of intangible heritage traces it back to Japan and Southeast Asia; it is a relative latecomer to Europe and the Americas. Formally recognized by the international community only in 2003, intangible heritage is, however, highly communicable. In the decade that has passed, intangible heritage has been diagnosed in 160 of the world's 195 states.

Epilogue: You Can't Make This Stuff Up!

ICH has entered the food chain:

> Flemish culture minister Joke Schauvliege has added the region's frieten, or french fry, culture to the government's list of intangible cultural heritage. Last week the minister received a petition signed by supporters of Navefri, the national association of french fry shops, for the friet culture to be listed. . . . The recognition covers the knowledge and traditions of the *friet* culture, but also the famed *frietkot*—those roadside stands, often of eye-catching design, where *frieten* are sold with all the trimmings. "Fry shops have been an everyday thing for so long that there wasn't any interest in them anymore," said Navefri chair Bernard Lefèvre. "It was thanks to the interest shown by foreigners that we started realising their value. We now have to ensure they carry on existing." (Hope 2014)

References Cited

Espada, Arcadi. 2004. "Entrevista de Arcadi Espada a Juan Goytisolo." *La espía del sur.* http://web.archive.org/web/20050516010332/http://www.geocities.com/laespia/goytisolo2.htm.

Foster, Michael Dylan. 2011. "The UNESCO Effect: Confidence, Defamiliarization, and a New Element in the Discourse on a Japanese Island." *Journal of Folklore Research* 48 (1): 63–107.

Hafstein, Valdimar Tr. 2009. "Intangible Heritage as a List: From the Masterpieces to Representation." In *Intangible Heritage*, edited by Laurajane Smith and Natsuko Akagawa, 93–111. New York: Routledge.

———. 2012. "Cultural Heritage." In *A Companion to Folklore*, edited by Regina F. Bendix and Galit Hasan-Rokem, 500–19. Malden, MA: Wiley-Blackwell.

———. 2014. "Protection as Dispossession: Government in the Vernacular." In *Cultural Heritage in Transit: Intangible Rights as Human Rights*, edited by Deborah Kapchan, 25–57. Philadelphia: University of Pennsylvania Press.

Hope, Alan. 2014. "Frietkoten Recognised as Cultural Heritage." *Flanders Today,* January 13. http://www.flanderstoday.eu/living/frietkoten-recognised-cultural-heritage.

Kapchan, Deborah. 2014. "Intangible Heritage in Transit: Goytisolo's Rescue and Moroccan Cultural Rights." In *Cultural Heritage in Transit: Intangible Rights as Human Rights*, edited by Deborah Kapchan, 177–94. Philadelphia: University of Pennsylvania Press.

Kirshenblatt-Gimblett, Barbara. 1995. "Theorizing Heritage." *Ethnomusicology* 39 (3): 367–80.

———. 1998. *Destination Culture: Tourism, Museums, and Heritage.* Berkeley: University of California Press.

Lowthorp, Leah. 2013. "Scenarios of Endangered Culture, Shifting Cosmopolitanisms: Kutiyattam and UNESCO Intangible Cultural Heritage in Kerala, India." PhD diss., University of Pennsylvania.

Noyes, Dorothy. 2006. "The Judgment of Solomon: Global Protections for Tradition and the Problem of Community Ownership." *Cultural Analysis* 5:27–56.

Poulot, Dominique. 2006. *Une histoire du patrimoine en Occident.* Paris: Presses Universitaires de France.

Silverman, Carol. 2014. "Balkan Romani Culture, Human Rights, and the State: Whose Heritage?" In *Cultural Heritage in Transit: Intangible Rights as Human Rights*, edited by Deborah Kapchan, 125–47. Philadelphia: University of Pennsylvania Press.

UNESCO. 2008. UNESCOPRESS Press Release No. 112, May 11.

Wittgenstein, Ludwig. 2009. *Philosophical Investigations.* 4th edition. Translated and edited by P. M. S. Hacker and Joachim Schulte. Oxford: Wiley-Blackwell.

VALDIMAR TR. HAFSTEIN is Associate Professor of Folkloristics and Ethnology at the University of Iceland, a KNAW visiting professor at the Meertens Institute, Amsterdam, and a visiting researcher at the Department of Conservation of the University of Gothenburg, Sweden. He chaired Iceland's National UNESCO Commission from 2011–12 and now serves as the president of SIEF (International Society for Ethnology and Folklore).

9   From Cultural Forms to Policy Objects: Comparison in Scholarship and Policy

THIS WELCOME EDITED collection is concerned not only with intangible cultural heritage (ICH), which has commandeered our field's attention for the past decade, but with comparison, about which we really ought to talk more. Folklorists today rarely launch comparative inquiry top-down, from the etic categories of early genre theory. Nor has a comprehensive practice of bottom-up comparison emerged from the turn to emic categories and the ethnography of communication at the local level. Rather, the editors here have formalized and made explicit a third turn. Comparison today is apt to move sideways to a category of policy, intangible cultural heritage, and its putative instantiations, the "elements" that get listed and receive safeguarding. Despite emerging from political debate rather than academic discussion, these new policy objects bear a conspicuous resemblance to the stuff we know as folklore.

Comparison in Scholarship and Policy

Of course this is no accident. The UNESCO conversation draws on earlier conversations in folklore studies. Like folklore studies, heritage policy draws on the longer and broader sociocultural work of modernity in singling out local traditions as identity markers. This work is bound up with both nation-state formation and regional or ethnic resistances to it. The social, political, academic, and policy lines of attention to traditional expression have been inextricably intertwined for at least four hundred years.[1] But this intertwining excites considerable anxiety among folklore scholars. All of our efforts to reform ourselves and deconstruct others cannot pull us out of this tangle into the heroic isolation proper to objective social inquiry. Hence, there is a second layer of comparison implicit in much academic work on

161

cultural policy and indeed cultural politics: reversing Ginzburg (1990), we might call it negative abduction. Instead of drawing conclusions about folkloristic concept-building from looking over to the case of heritage policy, we tend rather to pull away from parallelisms that to outsiders often look like convergence or simple identity. What *we* do as scholars is not what *they* do as heritage bureaucrats! (To be sure, we may also attempt to align ourselves with local-level activisms and insights, or in moments of professional necessity argue for the utility of convergence with UNESCO and/or the state.) To study heritage production is to place ourselves on a different plane.[2]

Like any intellectual field, however, and particularly like folklore studies, heritage policy performs comparison to constitute its object. As Barbara Kirshenblatt-Gimblett (2004) pointed out in the early stages of the ICH juggernaut, the category, once invented, generates its own content. More immediately, it recruits amenable phenomena. By virtue of being hailed into ICH, cultural forms are transformed into comparable objects. When Prince UNESCO comes calling, the slipper must be made to fit a disappearing local dialect, a vibrant communal festival, a suspect healing ritual, a court dance, a style of mask: phenomena at different scales, differently embedded in social life, different in status and visibility, now become the same kind of thing.

The category of ICH does not only generate comparability but itself emerged from recurrent and cumulative acts of comparison. Such a policy process takes its empirical point of departure from a critical situation that actors seek to address. To make the case for addressing the immediate problem, however, the policy initiative must attach itself to what Kenneth Burke (1945) calls a *representative anecdote*. The representative anecdote is treated as an exemplar of its category, but it in fact guides the category formation in the first place. It is used to facilitate the recognition and legitimation of both the critical situation and all future comparanda.

In the West the representative anecdote of valorized oral tradition is Homer, such that oral tradition can hardly be conceived without the narrative of regional variation and proto-national convergence that shaped the Homeric texts. It is not surprising that Homer is regularly invoked in Juan Goytisolo's early discussions of the *hlayqiya* storytellers of Jemaa el-Fna square, Marrakesh, the founding instance of the Masterpiece program (e.g., 2001). Indeed, Goytisolo weaves a complex comparative mesh to address his critical situation, a proposed commercial development next to the square. He looks back in time, sideways in culture, upward in literary status, and upward in discourse genres to make his case. Goytisolo can draw a straight line from the hlayqiya back to an Arabic great tradition by invoking their performances of content from the *Thousand and One Nights* and the epic of the Antariyya. He also refers to Homeric epic, Vedic hymns, biblical narrative, chansons de geste, the *Libro de Buen Amor,* and other European medieval texts as parallel modes of storytelling, oral in their origins if not in the form they have reached the present. He points upward to the valorization of oral storytelling by canonical authors such as Cervantes and, of course, himself; he also calls in the scholarly validation of such traditions by theorists such as Ong, Parry, and Bakhtin. He remarks on the resistant oralities that allowed the work of poets such as Mandelstam to survive censorship and the "latent oralities" of the literary avant-garde from Joyce forward. In short, he constructs a robust class of oral expression that can encompass the activities of the hlayqiya. He bolsters their precarious position by drawing on the highest-status comparanda available, oralizing the canon in order to canonize the oral. The trace of this operation of ennoblement (Bourdieu 1991) can be seen in the honorific label "oral literature." Once the new category is secured, it can safely populate itself by recruiting further low-status members.

The work of comparison generates the carapace of cultural objects (Urban 1999; cf. Noyes 2005). As we see from the case of Jemaa el-Fna, the hardest objects emerge when the work of comparison is driven by rhetorical need, the desire to fix mutable phenomena within existing frameworks so that they can be administered or manipulated through available means (Burke 1945; Fernandez 1986). Thus "oral literature" becomes a special case of literature *tout court*, intangible cultural heritage safeguarding is calqued upon material heritage preservation, and, in a related sphere of cultural policy, "cultural property" rights are modeled on individual intellectual property rights. A range of consequences ensue from such object generation. One is that modern Western exceptions are transformed into general rules, the unmarked or generic alternative to the special cases of everything that happens in the rest of the world and the rest of history. Another is *Rücklauf,* the afterlife of discarded academic concepts in other zones of social practice (Bendix and Welz 1999), as when "authenticity" becomes a central criterion for ICH listing.

Once constructed, cultural objects cannot be uncreated or even easily re-formed. When we cast aside old ideas, old policies, and old representations they do not decay but continue as rubbish at the margins of our attention, perhaps to be reinhabited by new actors and agendas, as abandoned shells are reanimated by hermit crabs (Thompson 1979). This is one reason for the field's ongoing anxiety about comparison and the theory it generates. But there is really no choice: comparing is how we think (Urban 1999; Gingrich and Fox 2002).

This volume takes a modest approach. It sets up comparison as heuristic or essay: a trying-out of insights by imposing a common but temporary framework of analysis. In this case, to torture the metaphor further, comparison provides not a durable housing but a momentary shelter, which becomes the point of departure for the next phase of analysis. As the case studies are viewed under the present conceptual roof, new analytical issues will emerge, allowing the cases to regroup and diverge as they move down the road toward their next way stations. The forthcoming shelters that I can perceive have a familiar look to them (for inquiry rarely proceeds in a straight line toward the horizon of the wholly new, but loops and retraces and revises): liberal modernity, the state, international norms, and face-to-face interaction.

Liberal Modernization and the Unmooring of Cultural Forms

The "elements" of ICH addressed in these pages can be sorted roughly into specialist practices and participatory communal celebrations, allowing for the frequent framing of the former within the latter. These two kinds of performance respond somewhat differently to the cultural work of modernization—that is, to the reconfiguration of the forms of life through rationalization and standardization in the interest of efficiency. This process includes the large-scale transformation of a growing scope of forms of life into what I have above called *cultural objects*. By a *form* I mean a concentrated, situated area of practice that is continually reproduced and tacitly recognized insofar as it belongs to the competence of a network of actors; in plain English, it is something people know *to* do and know *how* to do. In folkloristic terms, form is sometimes realized in per-formance, practice that "assumes responsibility for a display of communicative competence to an audience"

(Hymes 1974). A form can also precipitate a cultural object when it receives focused, explicit recognition and interpretation, beginning with the attaching of a label. Parallel to, intertwined with, or even supplanting the ongoing recreation of the form, the new object is sustained through active effort, management, and debate, which may be further hardened into institutional reproduction. ICH is only one of many objects thrown off from practice in the history of modernity,[3] and a given form—say the tarantella of southern Italy—can readily circulate among such categories as ICH, regional resistance, world music, new age spirituality, feminist performance, tourist entertainment, and exercise routine while still being practiced locally in less explicit frameworks (Inserra forthcoming). When hitherto indeterminate forms are recruited into defined objects such as ICH, one result is what Foster (2011) calls the "UNESCO effect" of defamiliarization: a fall into modernity that facilitates the alienation of practices, for both good and ill depending on the case and point of view.

The Kutiyattam actors, Cheju shamans, Vimbuza healers, and Roma musicians of this volume are specialists insofar as they have trained and worked over a long period to master practices that are not accessible to everyone. They are sought out for their skills by members of their communities and compete among themselves to build their reputations and their client base. As is often the case with traditional specialists, these four groups are socially marginal, and they hope that UNESCO or other outside recognition will afford them a rise in status along with a rise in income. In the case of Kerala, with the creation of the Kutiyattam Kendra, both elevations have been accomplished for at least some well-placed actors. Another hope entertained is that the practice itself, once valorized as heritage, can benefit from professionalization via either market or institutional mechanisms. Lowthorp shows that this outcome is ambiguous in Kerala, where older connoisseurs feel that the art has been cheapened by its growing visibility. The Cheju shamans from the island are assumed to be too expensive now that they are recognized, and other practitioners from the mainland are taking some of their business away. The Vimbuza healers are still waiting to have their conception of spiritual illness acknowledged; the proposed measures for safeguarding the tradition seem rather to place a containment wall around it, with the training of practitioners in "intellectual property rights, health issues associated with HIV/AIDS prevention, relationships between traditional healers and 'modern medical practitioners,' gender issues, and the value of formal education" (Gilman, p. 66).

More generally, these specialist practitioners struggle against better-endowed competitors in a climate of liberal consumer choice. The UNESCO process sometimes assists and sometimes impedes the struggle, but greater forces are at work. The slow-paced Kutiyattam is not a preferred entertainment among busy Kerala entrepreneurs, just as the Cheju Yŏngdŭng Rite does not stand up well to K-pop in the eyes of a young audience. UNESCO recognition does not suffice to confer legitimacy on the Cheju shamans or the Malawi healers as efficacious practitioners on their own terms. Condemned by both Western medicine and Christianity, their activities must be relocated to the available domain of tourism. In general, practitioners can neither choose their market nor count on competing successfully within it. The Roma musicians are an exceptional case here, competing effectively insofar as market mechanisms are in operation but actively hindered by state politics and popular prejudice, which are given unwitting legitimation by the UNESCO discourse. The logic of competition operates also at the moment of practitioner recruitment: the intellectual abilities required to become a great Kutiyattam performer can be more lucratively exercised in India's booming tech economy, Lowthorp observes. Here again the Roma provide an exception, remaining musical specialists in part because social discrimination forecloses other life options.

The Macedonian wedding ritual as a whole and the Teškoto dance on a smaller scale, the Toshidon house-visiting, the Hongtong pilgrimage, and, to some extent, the Cheju Yŏngdŭng Rite operate by a somewhat different logic. They are participatory communal traditions, directly depending on a critical mass of committed participants for the reproduction of both competence and meaning. Although individuals can move in and out of central roles in the course of a life cycle without special apprenticeships, the practice as a whole depends as much upon the community of beneficiaries as on the immediate performers. With emigration, as in Macedonia, the collapse of a traditional industry such as the women's diving in Cheju, or most poignantly the disappearance of children, as in the Koshiki Archipelago, there may be little alternative to staged folklorization or, at best, touristification and recoding. Within a prospering and populated China, on the contrary, the Hongtong example shows a struggle for control of a vital tradition, comparable to other cases in which a practice is arbitrarily delineated geographically to exclude competing claims (Tauschek 2010; cf. Ballacchino 2012). But here too, with too much rather than too little attention, a top-down mode of management is likely to assert itself and sap the immediate practitioners' sense of responsibility to maintain the practice (Noyes 2006).

As innumerable commentators have observed, safeguarding does not guarantee the social base of either specialist practices or communal traditions. Moreover, the possibility that the social base might shift of its own accord is not taken into account by the UNESCO framing. When practitioners migrate and disperse from the country to the city, or their everyday circumstances are otherwise transformed, this does not entail the disappearance of their practices, which can be adapted in myriad ways to a new environment: professionalized, remediated, hybridized. One has only to think of the history of American popular music, as for example in the trajectories of blues and bluegrass (Cantwell 2008). Such relocations and blendings are invisible to the ICH ideology, which attaches art to emplaced community and imagines stasis of both persons and traditions as the default. This denies the fundamental logic of practice in the contemporary world, where, in Albert O. Hirschman's (1970) terms, exit trumps voice and loyalty: economic strategies and incentives frequently override both political motivations and particular attachments.

The Durable State

And yet, as far as these studies go, the state still appears to be the primary determinant of the ICH process in practice (Bendix, Eggert, and Peselmann 2012). "UNESCO is like a rain that comes and goes suddenly," as one of the Kutiyattam artists remarks (Lowthorp, p. 25). Indeed, UNESCO itself remains largely offstage, especially after the replacement of the Masterpieces program by the Representative List. States mediate the entire process. States have the monopoly of the intellectual resources required for producing a nomination, as several authors here note (although, as in Hongtong, it is often the locals who pay the bill). States represent the local level to UNESCO and vice-versa. States propose and then implement the safeguarding measures. In a Kafkaesque moment one would be tempted to conclude that neither UNESCO nor local communities exist at all except as enabling fictions of state bureaucracy. Forever examining the dialectic of global and local, observers tend to ignore the ongoing weight of the nation-state as a primary constraint upon, even generator of, smaller-scale agencies in cultural matters. The incentives and occasional resources provided by UNESCO are drawn into existing negotiations and interactions between states, local authorities, and citizens.

The variable outcomes of these case studies might be plotted around two axes: political framework (more liberal versus more statist) and degree of state capacity. The two factors interact to influence (rather than determine) both the intensity and the efficacy of intervention. Reading in this fashion, as an Anglo-American economist might, one is not surprised to see that the Japanese case offers, at least for the moment, the happiest local relationship to UNESCO recognition. There is heightened public interest in the Toshidon tradition but no active state intervention. The islanders have no extraordinary expectations from recognition nor are they traumatized by it; they are preoccupied, we might say appropriately, with the broader imagination of their future. The state occupies itself more usefully in the provision of infrastructures for the island, and while the liberal economist might deride the inefficiency of these job-creating construction projects, they can also be seen from Amartya Sen's (1999) point of view as creating "capabilities" for the islanders to remain and live the lives they choose.

Korea takes state paternalism further in addressing its peripheral regions and has actively intervened in safeguarding Cheju shamanism, with disruptive consequences. Its state-sponsored culture brokers bully the shaman's association into unrealistic preparations for nonexistent global visitors. Malawi, with a far lower state capacity, has similar ambitions for leveraging tradition into touristic development, and Gilman points to the development of a state cultural apparatus as the most (literally) constructive outcome of Vimbuza recognition, though one may wonder who will benefit most from its future interventions. In both cases state development agendas override local and practitioner wishes; in both cases the recognized tradition is promoted as exotic dance while local tensions over its status as instrumental ritual go unresolved.

China and Macedonia offer a similar parallel of comparable agendas across differing state capacities. China's concern with the "harmonization" of different societal elements offers a more sophisticated project of cultural hegemony than Macedonia's state nationalism. Placing extensive state resources into the ICH game, China can make effective pitches to UNESCO, while Macedonia, by Silverman's showing, has resorted to old templates, seeing the family resemblance but failing to recognize the critical differences between socialist-era state folklore and the UNESCO discourse. As in Malawi, moreover, in Macedonia a weak state is forced to put forward the most obvious candidates rather than the forms that might actually benefit from safeguarding. But China's greater capacity does not lead to reduced conflict on the ground. On the contrary, its empowerment of local brokers in Hongtong leads, even more than on Cheju, to division, resentment, and outright acts of cooption within the region. To be sure, the presence of a vigorous local population—a critical mass of committed participants—saves the Hongtong pilgrimages from the staged-folklore paradigm that so often seems the inevitable outcome of a safeguarding intervention.

In Kerala a strong state intervention takes a different form. This is not the state folklore ensemble as seen in Macedonia but, for a tradition that was already staged, a conservatory system: the Kutiyattam Kendra that oversees and subsidizes the training of new artists. Given the rise in artists' status and income, we could see this as the positive case for efficacious intervention from a high-capacity state—were it not that Lowthorp signals the widespread perception of the "Kerala model" as sclerotic or, in any case, as objectively undermined by the strong neoliberal turn in India overall. We must add that in every case of state intervention documented here, the exclusion of some practitioners has followed.

There is something about the ICH process that stirs my inner Anglo-American liberal, and I need to think this over. I do not oppose state support for culture—the state-supported opera houses of Europe, for example, are one of the joys of my life—but the asymmetries of ICH intervention are another matter. In the absence of state projects for social justice, cultural equity seems a mere formality. Then too, in the context of increasingly free global capital, state intervention is rarely more than a cosmetic response to deepening structural violence.

Still, given the human scale at which we have to live, given our desire to sustain the world as we know it within the temporal and spatial horizons available to us, active management is unavoidable. Silverman and Gilman both raise the possibility of better-designed interventions that could emerge from a clearer understanding of local-level challenges via a more democratic dialogue. Should we hope and try for this? In this edited collection, as in the ICH literature as a whole, there is no obvious way out of neoliberalism, that massively powerful hybrid of global capital and the nation-state. The latter has proven an extraordinarily resilient cultural object, which neither internationalist nor localist activism have done much to re-form. Are we stuck here?

The Limits of International Norms

The essays suggest two ways out. Local authorities or activists frequently pitch UNESCO as a deus ex machina that will rescue the regional economy. Practitioners hold the more immediate hope that UNESCO will raise their income. Both sets of expectations are routinely disappointed.

But there are also recurrences here of UNESCO as spurring a different kind of "global dream" (Yun 2006): the fantasy of recognition, participation, dignity. People and their practices will meet on equal ground or at least sit at the same table (the latter metaphor offers the more concrete hope, for getting to Geneva is easier than getting to Utopia). Silverman formulates a still more limited and potentially achievable aim: familiarizing people on the ground with the UNESCO discourse to give them leverage in their struggles with the state. This could be seen as a pragmatic scaling-down of a founding purpose of the United Nations: to disseminate norms.

Yet Silverman's own documentation of the situation of Roma in Macedonia and You's account of rural-urban inequality in China both give the reader pause, and the parallel domain of human rights does not inspire optimism for ICH. We have seen the widespread discrediting of human rights discourse as Western imperialism, and there has certainly been enough clueless intervention in the name of human rights to provide fodder for such critiques. Of course we cannot do without international norms, that is, norms as the tent under which conversation can take place and change can be fostered. International norms are demonstrably useful in constraining elites and pushing them in desired directions, as the end of apartheid in South Africa demonstrates (Klotz 1999). But they are not often the most useful tools for subaltern actors in their immediate struggles.

On the contrary, the Marxist suspicion of hegemonic promises is borne out by many instances of UNESCO on the ground. While local agencies certainly emerge in these negotiations, the arena is defined from above. Furthermore, there is a fundamental inequality not only of resources but of scale between the ground-level actors and the nation-states in which they operate. This is to say nothing of UNESCO itself. Representatives of that agency are unlikely to be on hand to back up traditional practitioners facing encroachment from regional entrepreneurs or state officials. Such encroachment is ubiquitous and goes largely unnoticed by anyone who is not directly affected. Let's face facts: for the foreseeable future, most subaltern practitioners and marginal communities are on their own. Is it possible for sympathetic scholars on the sidelines to imagine an intervention from below that would work not upon the local but upward—toward and beyond the state?

From Deus ex Machina to Dignity on the Ground: Back to the Future

Certainly we have imagined more useful assistance on the ground. In the United States, applied and public folklore agencies—the Philadelphia Folklore Project being the case I know best—have been extensively concerned with facilitating artist- and community-determined agendas. These include not only access to grant funding and performance venues but matters of material and social infrastructure such as the defense of neighborhoods against gentrification and the cultivation of workable intergroup relationships within urban populations under pressure. On ICH's own Ground Zero, the Jemaa el-Fna square of Marrakesh, Thomas Barone Beardslee (2014) has proposed Sen's capabilities approach as an alternative to ICH safeguarding. This could begin, Beardslee suggests, with collective bargaining power: the formation of a performers' association that would have standing to negotiate group health insurance rates, claim compensation for lost earnings during the periods when they are displaced by city-sponsored touristic events, and so forth.

Our field is in a position to insist on the social base of practice and has shown a remarkable capacity for improvisation, with public folklorists learning on the fly about the operations of small businesses and regional economies, the institutional and material infrastructures of local communities. Until quite recently, however, these issues have formed no part of the formal training of folklorists, at least in the United States, and we can claim no distinctive expertise in them. Does our historical disciplinary experience with the processes of expressive culture bring anything constructive to the problem?

I find clues from two instances in You's piece, in which face-to-face encounters redress the instabilities of scale-jumping between the local and the state. She describes how the conflict between villages over ownership of the Yao and Shun tradition was settled through a ritual carried out by the assembled temple associations. As she points out, a problem generated from above was resolved by a local-to-local process. Still more telling is the incident in which the drunken official, declaring his disdain for the community, was scolded by a "grandmother" in the audience. This brought him down to earth, as it were: the interpersonal operation of shaming had at least some force to override radical inequalities. Sometimes the state and the local meet face to face.

An old-school folkloristic approach to the problem—I am not saying it is the right approach or the only one—might conclude that the dream of global recognition is too far off the ground to be worth much of our time as analysts, policymakers, activists, or citizens. The table is not big enough for all of us to sit there. And the more network nodes between global and local partners, the more opportunities for alienation and deviation en route (Noyes 2003). The more representation, the more misrepresentation.

One corrective for these inevitable misconnections lies in the extent to which global actors still have local hinterlands. Sometimes representatives have to go home and meet the represented. This leverage of the grandmothers is diminishing, of course, with the increasing isolation of a transnational global elite that interact only with one another in spaces gated off from the populace. But even formal democracy at its most cynical affords some opportunities. Wherever there is performance there is the possibility of emergence. The most important arenas for recognition, participation, and dignity remain those at the human scale in which bodies encounter one another and actions excite and demand answering action: where respons-ibility cannot be deferred, deflected, or denied. While today every component of Ben-Amos's (1972) famous definition of folklore has been effectively challenged, as a whole the idea of "artistic communication in small groups" still has power to evoke the scale at which complex interaction and, not coincidentally, social control can operate most fully. Folklorists' studies of shared forms offer an important key to the coexistence of diverse interests in confined spaces over time. The ability to understand democracy on the ground—not formal representation but genuine interpersonal bargaining power—does not by itself solve local, much less global problems; we will have to move back upscale in some fashion. But the on-the-ground engagement is an essential, one might say foundational, component of any solution. It is the component to which folklorists are best equipped to contribute through their exercises in comparison.

Notes

1. I take the metaphor of intellectual activity as lines of inquiry that dovetail, entangle, bundle, diverge, and so on from Ingold 2010 and the conversations with Tim Ingold at the June 2014 "Featured Thinker Day" of the Zentrum für Theorie und Methodik der Kulturwissenschaften at the University of Göttingen.

2. Thinking it over, I realize that I myself am perhaps the field's most conspicuous practitioner of this mode of negative abduction, and for me disciplinary status anxiety is at its core.

3. I am recalling the derivation of "object" from the Latin verb *jacere*, to throw (cf. Ingold 2010, 345).

References Cited

Ballacchino, Katia. 2012. "Unity Makes . . . Intangible Heritage: Italy and Network Nomination." In *Heritage Regimes and the State*, edited by Regina F. Bendix, Aditya Eggert, and Arnika Peselmann, 121–40. Göttingen: Universitätsverlag Göttingen.

Beardslee, Thomas Barone. 2014. "Questioning Safeguarding: Heritage and Capabilities at the Jemaa el Fnaa." PhD diss., The Ohio State University.

Ben-Amos, Dan. 1972. "Toward a Definition of Folklore in Context." In *Toward New Perspectives in Folklore*, edited by Américo Paredes and Richard Bauman, 3–15. Austin: University of Texas Press.

Bendix, Regina F., Aditya Eggert, and Arnika Peselmann, eds. 2012. *Heritage Regimes and the State*. Göttingen: Universitätsverlag Göttingen.

Bendix, Regina F., and Gisela Welz, eds. 1999. "Cultural Brokerage: Forms of Intellectual Practice in Society." Special issue, *Journal of Folklore Research* 36 (2–3).

Bourdieu, Pierre. 1991. *Language and Symbolic Power*. Edited and introduced by John B. Thompson. Translated by Gino Raymond and Matthew Adamson. Cambridge, MA: Harvard University Press.

Burke, Kenneth. 1945. *A Grammar of Motives*. Berkeley: University of California Press.

Cantwell, Robert. 2008. *If Beale Street Could Talk: Music, Community, Culture*. Urbana: University of Illinois Press.

Fernandez, James W. 1986. *Persuasions and Performances: The Play of Tropes in Culture*. Bloomington: Indiana University Press.

Foster, Michael Dylan. 2011. "The UNESCO Effect: Confidence, Defamiliarization, and a New Element in the Discourse on a Japanese Island." *Journal of
Folklore Research* 48 (1): 63–107.

Gingrich, André, and Richard Fox. 2002. Introduction to *Anthropology by Comparison*, edited by André Gingrich and Richard Fox. London: Routledge.

Ginzburg, Carlo. 1990. *Clues, Myths, and the Historical Method.* Translated by John
and Ann Tedeschi. Baltimore: Johns Hopkins University Press.

Goytisolo, Juan. 2001. "Defending Threatened Cultures." Speech delivered at
the opening of the meeting of the Jury, Proclamation of Masterpieces of the
Oral and Intangible Patrimony of Humanity, May 15. http://www.unesco
.org/bpi/intangible_heritage/goytisoloe.htm.

Hirschman, Albert O. 1970. *Exit, Voice, and Loyalty: Responses to Decline in Firms,
Organizations, and States.* Cambridge MA: Harvard University Press.

Hymes, Dell. 1974. *Foundations in Sociolinguistics: An Ethnographic Approach.* Philadelphia: University of Pennsylvania Press.

Ingold, Tim. 2010. "Drawing Together: Materials, Gestures, Lines." In *Experiments
in Holism: Theory and Practice in Contemporary Anthropology*, edited by Tom Otto
and Nils Bubandt, 343–61. Oxford: Wiley-Blackwell.

Inserra, Incoronata. Forthcoming. *Reimagining the Italian South: The Tarantella
Music and Dance Revival from Italy to the US.* Urbana: University of Illinois Press.

Kirshenblatt-Gimblett, Barbara. 2004. "Intangible Heritage as Metacultural
Production." *Museum International* 56 (1–2): 52–65.

Klotz, Audie. 1999. *Norms in International Relations: The Struggle against Apartheid.*
Ithaca, NY: Cornell University Press.

Noyes, Dorothy. 2003. "Group." In *Eight Words for the Study of Expressive Culture*,
edited by Burt Feintuch, 7–41. Urbana: University of Illinois Press.

———. 2005. "On Sociocultural Categories." In "Folklore Abroad: On the Dif-
fusion and Revision of Sociocultural Categories," edited by Dorothy Noyes,
3–7. Special issue of *Indian Folklife* 19. http://indianfolklore.org/journals
/index.php/IFL/issue/view/47/showToc.

———. 2006. "The Judgment of Solomon: Global Protections for Tradition and
the Problem of Community Ownership." *Cultural Analysis* 5:27–56.

Sen, Amartya. 1999. *Development as Freedom.* New York: Knopf.

Tauschek, Markus. 2010. *Wertschöpfung aus der Tradition. Der Karneval von Binche
und die Konstituierung kulturellen Erbes.* Berlin: LIT Verlag.

Thompson, Michael. 1979. *Rubbish Theory: The Creation and Destruction of Value.*
Oxford: Oxford University Press.

Urban, Greg. 1999. "The Role of Comparison in the Light of the Theory of Culture." In *Critical Comparisons in Politics and Culture*, edited by John R. Bowen
and Roger Peterson, 90–109. Cambridge: Cambridge University Press.

Yun, Kyoim. 2006. "The 2002 World Cup and a Local Festival in Cheju: Global
Dreams and the Commodification of Shamanism." *Journal of Korean Studies*
11:7–40.

DOROTHY NOYES is Professor of English and Comparative Studies, core
faculty in the Center for Folklore Studies, and a research associate of

the Mershon Center for International Security Studies at The Ohio State University. A Fellow of the American Folklore Society, she is author of *Fire in the Plaça: Catalan Festival Politics after Franco* (University of Pennsylvania Press, 2003) and far too many theoretical essays. Her interests include the traditional public sphere in Romance-speaking Europe, the social organization of vernacular creativity, folk economic thought, and the role of culture concepts in international relations. She is working slowly on a book about political exemplarity.

Index

Page numbers in italics refer to figures.

action plans. *See* safeguarding
Aikawa-Faure, Noriko, 135
American Folklore Society, 7, 8, 12n11
audience, 48–49, 155
authenticity, 33, 44, 50, 85, 101, 102–3, 139, 144, 163

Beardslee, Thomas Barone, 171
Ben-Amos, Dan, 173
Bendix, Regina F., 8
Brown, Michael F., 126
Burke, Kenneth, 162

Cheju Island, South Korea, 41–43, *42*, 55n1, 155–56, 167
  See also simbang; South Korea; Yŏngdŭng Rite
Chen Yongchao, 118–19, 120
China, 126n4, 166–67, 168–69, 170
  heritage policy, 114, 117, 118, 119, 121, 139
  See also Hongtong County, China; Hongtong Zouqin Xisu
  comparison, 3, 8, 9, 34n7, 161–64, 173
Convention Concerning the Protection of the World Cultural and Natural Heritage (1972). *See under* UNESCO: legal instruments
Convention for the Safeguarding of the Intangible Cultural Heritage (2003). *See under* UNESCO: legal instruments
Convention on the Protection and Promotion of the Diversity of Cultural Expressions (2005). *See under* UNESCO: legal instruments
Čučkov, Manoil, 96, 98
cultural policy. *See* intangible cultural heritage: policy

Dalmia, Vasudha, 23
De Cesari, Chiara, 11n4, 125
defamiliarization, 86–87, 165
development, 17–19, 30–32, 34n5, 73–74, 93, 167
  effect on ICH, 52–53, 78, 81, 84–85, 87, 101, 104–5, 146, 152, 155, 166
  See also globalization; modernization; tourism
Dunin, Elsie, 97, 98, 99, 109n6

economic development. *See* development
Eggert, Aditya, 8
ethnicity, 68, 94–96, 102, 106, 108

folkloristics, 2, 3, 7–8, 12n11, 34n7, 103, 161–62, 171–73
Former Yugoslav Republic of Macedonia (FYROM). *See* Macedonia
Foster, Michael Dylan, 7, 131, 137–38, 152, 155–56, 165

Galičnik wedding
  ICH application, 100–103, 107
  participants, 101–3, 152, 166–67
  safeguarding, 101–2, 106, 149–50, 151
  See also Teškoto
Gilman, Lisa, 7, 134, 136–37, 145–46, 150, 151, 152, 168, 169
globalization, 30, 32, 33, 146
  See also development; modernization
Goytisolo, Juan, 154–55, 162–63
Grant, Catherine, 102
Gule Wamkulu, 65, 71, 73, 75n2
  See also Vimbuza

Hafstein, Valdimar Tr., 8, 10
heritage regimes, 8, 52, 125
Hirschman, Albert O., 167
Hongtong County, China, 113–14, *114*
  See also China; Hongtong Zouqin Xisu
Hongtong Zouqin Xisu, 113, 114–18, *115*, 169
  funding, 121–22, 124, 127n8, 152, 167
  Hongtong Center for the Safeguarding of ICH, 119, 120–21, 124, 125, 150
  ICH application, 118–20, 122–23, 124–26, 127n8, 156
  participants, 116–18, 122–23, 166–67
  safeguarding, 118, 122, 123, 124–25
  shè (temple reconstruction associations), 117–18, 121–22, 123, 124–25, 172
Howard, Keith, 140

India, 17, 19, 30, 166
  heritage policy, 22–24, 27, 32, 158
  See also Kerala, India; Kutiyattam
  intangible cultural heritage, 2, 96, 102, 149–50

CPSIA information can be obtained
at www.ICGtesting.com
Printed in the USA
LVOW04s1437230216

476361LV00014B/151/P